DEEP CHANGE LEADERSHIP

A Model for Renewing and Strengthening ***Schools*** *and* ***Districts***

DOUGLAS REEVES

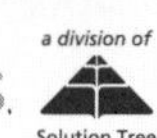

555 North Morton Street
Bloomington, IN 47404
800.733.6786 (toll free) / 812.336.7700
FAX: 812.336.7790

email: info@SolutionTree.com
SolutionTree.com

Printed in the United States of America

Library of Congress Cataloging-in-Publication Data

Names: Reeves, Douglas B., 1953- author.
Title: Deep change leadership : a model for renewing and strengthening schools and districts / Douglas Reeves.
Description: Bloomington, IN : Solution Tree Press, 2021. | Includes bibliographical references and index.
Identifiers: LCCN 2020037474 (print) | LCCN 2020037475 (ebook) | ISBN 9781952812071 (paperback) | ISBN 9781952812088 (ebook)
Subjects: LCSH: Educational leadership--United States. | Educational change--United States. | School management and organization--United States. | School districts--United States--Administration.,
Classification: LCC LB2805 .R4155 2021 (print) | LCC LB2805 (ebook) | DDC 371.200973--dc23
LC record available at https://lccn.loc.gov/2020037474
LC ebook record available at https://lccn.loc.gov/2020037475

Solution Tree
Jeffrey C. Jones, CEO
Edmund M. Ackerman, President

Solution Tree Press
President and Publisher: Douglas M. Rife
Associate Publisher: Sarah Payne-Mills
Art Director: Rian Anderson
Managing Production Editor: Kendra Slayton
Copy Chief: Jessi Finn
Production and Copy Editor: Rita Carlberg
Content Development Specialist: Amy Rubenstein
Proofreader: Sarah Ludwig
Text and Cover Designer: Kelsey Hergül
Editorial Assistants: Sarah Ludwig and Elijah Oates

For Bob Eaker, who exemplifies the values of leadership, learning, and friendship

Acknowledgments

The reference list is an inadequate way to express my intellectual debt to these particular scholars, who have shaped my thinking for this book: Albert-László Barabási, Luis Cruz, Jennifer Eberhardt, Amy Edmondson, Michael Fullan, Tom Guskey, John Hattie, Eric Kaufmann, John Kotter, Kim Marshall, Anthony Muhammad, and Ken Williams.

In addition, my colleagues at Creative Leadership Solutions are a continuing source of inspiration and support as they help schools around the world focus on what matters most. I express my particular appreciation to Lisa Almeida, Lauren Mahoney, Tony Flach, and Bill Sternberg.

My colleagues at the Institute of Coaching, an affiliate of the Harvard Medical School, have offered invaluable research and insights on how effective coaching leads to changes in individuals and organizations. I particularly acknowledge the work of Carol Kauffman and the executive coaches around the world who are part of the IOC Friday-morning huddle.

Solution Tree Press has been my partner for more than two decades, and its impact on education around the world is an example for every organization to follow. In particular, I appreciate the friendship and wisdom of Jeff Jones, CEO, and Douglas Rife, publisher and president of Solution Tree International.

Kendra Slayton, Rita Carlberg, and Amy Rubenstein provided insights and challenges that made this a better book and a more relevant contribution to the literature than it might have been had I been left to my own devices. Their contributions extend far beyond editing and are an intellectual partnership on which the success of this book depends.

Any errors and omissions are mine alone.

Solution Tree Press would like to thank the following reviewers:

Rick Bell
Assistant Principal
New Prague Middle School
New Prague, Minnesota

Libby Bonesteel
Superintendent
Montpelier Roxbury Public Schools
Montpelier, Vermont

Kalum McKay
Principal
Reagan Elementary School
Big Lake, Texas

Bruce Preston
Assistant Superintendent of
Curriculum and Personnel
Howell Township Public Schools
Howell, New Jersey

Matthew Treadway
Principal
Freedom Elementary School
Shepherdsville, Kentucky

Table of Contents

About the Author

Douglas Reeves, PhD, is the author of more than forty books and one hundred articles on leadership and organizational effectiveness. Twice named to the Harvard University Distinguished Authors Series, Dr. Reeves has worked with education and nonprofit organizations in fifty U.S. states and more than forty countries. Dr. Reeves's volunteer activities include service as the founding editor and co-publisher of *The SNAFU Review*, a collection of essays, stories, poetry, and art by disabled veterans. He is also the founder of the Marsh Writers Collaborative, an open forum for writers encouraging writers, as well as Finish the Dissertation, which provides free and noncommercial help to writers and doctoral candidates around the world. Dr. Reeves is a fellow of the Institute of Coaching, an affiliate of the Harvard Medical School.

To learn more about the work of Dr. Reeves, visit Creative Leadership Solutions at https://creativeleadership.net, or follow @DouglasReeves on Twitter.

To book Douglas Reeves for professional development, contact pd@SolutionTree.com.

Introduction

It's time for a change in change leadership. Having confronted a global pandemic and an economic crisis in 2020, as well as an international educational crisis emerging in the wake of these challenges, we must consider not whether to change but how best to lead inevitable change. The worst-possible leadership action as the pandemic recedes would be to say, "Thank goodness that's over; now we can go back to where we were before." The only question is whether the changes in change leadership will be deliberate—the result of a combination of our values and the best available evidence—or whether the changes will be chaotic.

Well before the pandemic of 2020, it was clear that most organizational-change efforts failed; that is, the pandemic alone did not create the need for a new model of change leadership. Changes in technology, students' needs, and growing competition in education require leaders and educators to engage in changes from the classroom to the boardroom at an accelerated level. Nevertheless, too many educational leaders in the 21st century persist in strategic-planning models that were designed for 20th century challenges. The economic and public health challenges of 2020 only revealed the weaknesses in these outdated and ineffective change models. It should not require another crisis for leaders to seize the opportunity to apply new models of change leadership for the challenges that lie ahead.

Why do organizational change generally and educational change specifically have such a poor track record? The problem is not a lack of literature on the subject. In the early days of 2020, Amazon listed more than three hundred thousand titles associated with *change* and more than one hundred thousand with *change leadership*. More than forty thousand of those titles were associated with educational change. But with all the literal and virtual ink spilled on the subject, we clearly have not made much progress. Since the 1980s, the leading scholar on organizational change has been Harvard Business School professor John P. Kotter. In *A Sense of Urgency*, Professor Kotter (2008) estimates that more than 70 percent of organizational-change efforts fail, and fewer than 10 percent of organizational-change efforts are implemented as intended. It's not just the abysmal failure rate of change efforts that should ring the alarm for a new model of change. The economic environment, workforce, and global economic structure combine to create challenges dramatically greater than those for which the 20th century change models were designed.

While we often believe that teachers and educational leaders seek the latest innovations and are more willing to change than organizations outside of education, a walk down the hallways of so many schools—and I have been involved in thousands of them—provides glimpses into classrooms in which desks are in rows and teachers speak from the front of the room, a configuration not different from that of the early 20th century. Even with 21st century technology widely used in schools and the pervasiveness of SMART Boards, projectors, and student-held devices, the foundations of teacher-student interaction remain stubbornly unchanged. In 2020, when substantial sums were poured into hardware and connectivity for students, instructional practices remained consistent with the past. A lecture on Zoom and other platforms is still a lecture, indistinguishable from that of ancient educational practice. The same is true of educational leaders' meetings, with presentations rather than deliberation and inquiry dominating school leadership teams, cabinet meetings, and board meetings. Technology, in sum, can create the illusion of change but not the reality of change.

Even as cognitive science has provided new insights into the best practices for teaching and learning, many parts of our profession remain stubbornly indifferent to the research. The prevailing model in schools I have observed is that even when change has clear and obvious advantages, such as improved reading performance for elementary school students or better engagement of secondary students, the application of teaching and leadership strategies that would produce such outcomes is largely voluntary. That has not deterred the publication of numerous books about change, many of which depend on a 20th century model of change that demonstrably does not work. For example, ask ten of your colleagues,

"What is necessary in order for us to have successful organizational change?" More than half will say *buy-in* or some equivalent term. But remember that even as the number of deaths attributable to COVID-19 rose precipitously during 2020, a substantial number of people elected not to change their habits, going mask-free and gathering with others in close proximity. This type of behavior is precisely what journalist Alan Deutschman (2007) finds has afflicted humans for decades. Whether the change is to stop smoking and start exercising after a heart attack, quit pursuing a student motivation strategy that demotivates students, or minimize one's exposure to a deadly and contagious virus, many people do not want to change. The evidence at the heart of this book is that such people are not going to readily provide the buy-in that traditional change models have pursued any more than they will listen to their physicians, students, or spouses. At this writing, according to the Insurance Institute for Highway Safety (2020), forty-eight U.S. states have laws outlawing texting while driving, yet it is not uncommon to see distracted drivers on their phones run through red lights as students prepare to cross the street. If a global pandemic and hundreds of thousands of deaths couldn't convince some people to wear masks and maintain social distancing, then state laws and the deaths of a few pedestrians will not stop the people at the downtown Boston intersection of Beacon Street and Mugar Way from texting while driving.

The good news is that we can do better. Schools can change, even in cases of reluctance and resistance, and they can do so with a model of *deep change leadership*. The path of deep change is clarity, both in terms of creating a compelling vision for change and in terms of helping staff members engage in change rather than become the victims of it. Teachers and building administrators—the people on the front lines of change—are often overwhelmed, overworked, and cynical about past failed change efforts. One of the keys to deep change is helping our colleagues understand what they can stop doing, a rarity in most change efforts. When leaders at every level, including teacher leaders, have clear and consistent evidence of the positive impact of change, then these efforts are sustained not with hierarchy but through the thoughtful pursuit of common goals and values.

What makes this book different? We will challenge strongly held traditional notions, such as the claim that buy-in from all stakeholders is essential for change, and replace these failed ideas not with autocratic and imperious demands from leaders but with practical models for engagement, inquiry, and action. We will explore why traditional change methods have failed and offer a compelling alternative. But first, let's delve into the research on effective leadership, familiarize ourselves with the model for deep change leadership, review the book's structure and contents, and consider the terminology around which the book is based—the true essence of the change leader.

THE RESEARCH ON EFFECTIVE CHANGE LEADERSHIP

I have drawn not only on the extensive research literature on change but also on my personal observations. In addition to teaching at every level—from elementary school to postdoctoral students—I have more than forty years of leadership experience in education, nonprofit, and governmental change-leadership efforts. This includes work in fifty U.S. states and more than forty countries across the world. While there are stark cultural differences from one part of the globe to another, there are striking consistencies with regard to the fundamental characteristics of effective leadership that form the foundation for individual, cultural, and organizational change. I have been lucky enough to observe these deep change strategies in the developing world, such as at the Zambian Leadership and Learning Institute, and at some of the world's most sophisticated educational and nonprofit organizations. These deep change strategies apply in impoverished areas such as Newark, New Jersey, and San Bernardino, California, and in economically elite environments such as Singapore and Silicon Valley, as well as in wealthy schools and communities around the world. In sum, what makes this book different is that it is broader than a sample size of one school's or district's journey; it includes a set of practices that can be applied in every school in which change is necessary.

The extensive reference list at the end of the book is my attempt to acknowledge my debt to scholars around the world who have thought deeply about change leadership. Their research on change in diverse fields, cultures, and locations offers a useful guide to readers who wish to explore the subject more thoroughly. But my job is not merely to review what has already been said about change leadership but rather to offer an explicit model for educational change, from an assessment of the organization's readiness for change to the implementation and sustainability of the change. The question of whether a new model is necessary can be answered with a single question: What works? Of all the educational change efforts you have seen, and perhaps led, what are the common elements of successful—and unsuccessful—change?

Since the passage of the No Child Left Behind Act (2002), educational policymakers have tested the hypothesis that piles of standards and mountains of assessments would improve educational results. The pervasive reliance on tests is common around the globe (Strauss, 2019). How many times do we need to test those hypotheses to determine that they are not supported by the evidence? If, after all, standards, high-stakes tests, and teacher evaluations based on raising student test scores are effective strategies, then student achievement twenty years after the passage of the No Child Left Behind Act should be significantly higher. But both national assessments, such as the National Assessment of Educational Progress, and international assessments, such as the Program for International Student Assessment, do not reflect these expected improvements in U.S. students, according to writers Graham Drake (2018) and Emily Richmond (2019), respectively. Even when the Every Student Succeeds Act (2015) liberated policymakers from many of the constraints of the No Child Left Behind Act, the vast majority of states continued to cling to demonstrably ineffective testing and evaluation practices (Reeves & Eaker, 2019). In a similar manner, according to professor Thomas R. Guskey (2020a), the vast majority of schools use grading and motivation practices in the third decade of the 21st century that were discredited by a century of research on the subject.

Very few scholars have challenged the traditional model of change, and educators and leaders owe a great debt to Guskey (2020b), whose important article on change also notes that the prevailing change-leadership emperors wear no clothes. And even Guskey, who is a friend and colleague of decades and who is as prolific a researcher and persuasive a speaker as the world of education has to offer, has witnessed one educational system after another applaud his presentations, agree with his work, and then do . . . nothing. In a personal conversation I had with Guskey, he noted that the scholarship since the 1940s has established that real change occurs not with rhetoric and buy-in but with practice and immediate—as short as two weeks—evidence of impact (T. Guskey, personal communication, July 8, 2020). In his extensive and widely replicated research on the subject, Guskey (2020b) has found that it is not training but short-term evidence of impact that makes the difference in implementation. In sum, we don't need new evidence or new communication techniques; we need a leadership model that will propel change from concept to implementation, not because it is popular but because it is essential.

Leaders want the *latest and best* for their schools, but their pursuit of the new shiny object too frequently leads to the abandonment of effective efforts just as they were taking hold. Why do such smart and dedicated leaders continue to move from one change to another without deep implementation? In my review of three dozen change efforts (Reeves, 2020c), I found that the schools and educational systems hit a frustration point before deep implementation took place. Complex tasks, whether they involve more-effective questioning techniques in the classroom, improved behavioral support processes, or technology integration, require practice and take time. In my review, I consistently found that deep implementation was associated with gains in student achievement. The problem that teachers and leaders faced, however, was that the gains in achievement were not composed of nice, linear stair-step results, with each improvement in implementation translating into associated gains in student achievement. In fact, there was little difference in gains among levels 1, 2, and 3 of implementation in terms of student performance. Only at the highest level—level 4—were gains significant. Unfortunately, when a school proceeds from level 1 to level 2 to level 3 and does not see results, faculty and leadership may conclude, "That didn't work; let's try another program." Thus, the chain of failed change initiatives continues. Raise the term *initiative fatigue* in any conversation, and you will see people nodding—perhaps wincing—in recognition. The solution to this dilemma is not to cast blame or challenge the motives of the administrators and faculty who initially supported failed change efforts. Rather, the solution is a new model of change, with practical steps to dramatically improve the probability that your next change effort—and there will be many in the years ahead—will succeed.

THE DEEP CHANGE LEADERSHIP MODEL

Deep change leadership is for everyone involved in educational change, including administrators, classroom educators, governing board members, and community leaders—all of whom share a common interest in designing and implementing effective change in schools. When change efforts are left solely to senior leaders, then faculty, staff, students, and those in the broader community inevitably feel that the change is at best irrelevant to their daily lives and at worst a sign of disrespect and distrust, alienating them from the joint vision that must be shared in order for change to take effect and be sustained. Deep change represents significant shifts in the way that we have traditionally designed and implemented change in schools and districts, and it calls for the following four fundamental leadership phases: (1) imagining, (2) focusing, (3) implementing, and (4) accelerating.

IMAGINING

Deep change requires leaders to create two compelling visions. The first is the positive vision that will represent the impact of change. For example, change that results in improved student academic performance yields a vision not just about test scores but about bright futures for the students, their families, and their communities. It's a vision that encompasses a better climate and culture in the classrooms, hallways, and streets. It's a vision in which the community takes pride in schools and advocates for the success of the entire system. The second vision represents what happens when we fail to change. When students do not succeed, they face lifetime consequences in employment and economic opportunities for themselves and their families. This bleak vision is as important as the positive vision, because when changes become difficult—as they always will—it is not just the pain of change but the pain of failing to change that leaders must consider. It is important to note that, unlike with traditional change efforts, these visions are not communicated in pursuit of buy-in. One of the greatest myths of traditional change leadership is that the leader must gain buy-in from the staff before proceeding with change. This book argues that staff engagement occurs not as a result of rhetoric but as a result of empirical results.

FOCUSING

While traditional change efforts are often associated with cumbersome strategic plans, deep change requires focus on a few—no more than six—priorities that will guide administrators, faculty, students, and community members (Reeves, 2016). Most importantly, deep change requires that leaders identify not only their areas of focus but also specific practices that they will stop. One of the greatest causes of failed change efforts is that they are piled on top of previous plans, initiatives, and mandates, while those responsible for implementing the change have no more time or resources than they had before the change efforts began.

IMPLEMENTING

One of the distinguishing characteristics of deep change is the explicit link between causes and effects. When leaders focus only on results—something that many take pride in doing—they are doomed to unsustainable change because it's often unclear if the results were associated with actions, strategy, or luck. Psychologist Maria Konnikova (2020) argues that leadership strategy is less like chess and more like poker. In chess, there is a theoretically perfect move for each player. But in poker, as in the real world, strategy and chance combine to yield results. A good decision can be accompanied by poor results because of factors that have nothing to do with the leader's actions. Just ask every educational leader who endured the spring of 2020, having found that the January's plans were scuttled by March of that year. Conversely, bad decisions can be accompanied by good results, and Konnikova (2020) reminds leaders they should be wary of self-congratulation when they were in fact luckier than they were savvy. While the role of chance cannot be eliminated from leadership decision making, the balance is most likely to be tilted in favor of the quality of leadership decisions when causes and effects are explicitly linked.

ACCELERATING

Deep change requires actions that yield short-term results. Rather than traditional multiyear plans, deep change will begin to show results in one hundred days, providing the energy and confidence that everyone needs to sustain change efforts over the long term.

Thus, deep change represents a significant and striking alternative to the change theories and practices that have dominated schools and other organizations. As the chapters that follow will demonstrate, deep change can be accomplished with great results not only for traditional educational measures but also for improved culture, climate, and engagement.

ABOUT THIS BOOK

The book is organized into three parts. In part 1, we explore the deep change imperative, beginning in chapter 1 with a discussion on why a new model of change is essential. In chapter 2, we consider the pain and difficulty inherent in change, and in chapter 3, we confront one of the principal impediments to change: the myth of universal buy-in. While universal buy-in is not necessary, leaders must create the essential antecedents to change, which include unmistakable evidence that both the individuals within the organization and the organization itself *are capable of change.* So in chapter 4, we'll preview the phases of deep change to help determine stakeholders' readiness. The essence of part 1 is that change is difficult—and any claim that leaders can magically remove impediments to change with just the right slogans, posters, or coffee mugs is simply not realistic or effective.

Part 2 introduces the what and the how of deep change leadership. Paradoxically, as we'll discuss in chapter 5, leaders must begin by deciding what will *not* change. Even in organizations that need significant cultural and operational change, there are remnants of values, traditions, and vital stories that can be preserved. Beginning with chapter 6, on imagining, we shift to an in-depth look at the phases of deep change. While much hot air has been expelled in the service of finding one's passion, as we'll find in chapter 6, the best evidence suggests that passion alone is a fool's errand. Rather, effective individual and organizational change requires passion with a purpose.

In our examination of the focusing phase of deep change in chapter 7, we find that if there is one constant in the litany of failed change efforts, it is fragmentation. This is exemplified in the strategic-planning industry, which generates an endless stream of goals, strategies, objectives, and tasks. Georgetown University computer science professor Cal Newport (2016b) demonstrates convincingly that the steady stream of distractions that characterize the work lives of most people in the 21st century undermines our ability to learn. This is true of students who think that they can multitask and of teachers and leaders who are never far from one or more devices as they attempt to give their full attention to students. Fragmentation is the enemy of focus, and that is why any change effort that does not explicitly identify what teachers and leaders can stop doing is doomed. While focus is rare and fragmentation is the rule, it is the exceptional leader who chooses focus over fragmentation. The organizations burdened by fragmentation are not governed by malicious leaders. These leaders genuinely want the best for their colleagues and organizations. The clear and convincing evidence is that the leaders who are willing to make the tough decisions to *focus*, to say *no* far more frequently than they say *yes*, will have the greatest opportunities for successful change. Veteran Silicon Valley executive Kim Scott (2019) tells of one of the most effective Apple executives she ever encountered who kept two notebooks in his office. One was exceptionally large and labeled *No*, and the other was exceedingly small and labeled *Yes*. The executive kept these rejected and green-lit design proposals in physical form so that when he dropped the *No* notebook with a thud, he was able to tell his employees that most ideas, including some particularly good ones, get rejected and to urge them not to take criticism and rejection personally. The lessons of the *No* notebook are what make the contents of the *Yes* notebook successful.

In chapter 8, we explore the implementing phase of deep change, with a focus on leading indicators and the leadership and learning matrix, the means by which change leaders can better understand the causes and the results of success and failures and ultimately make sounder learning-based decisions for their schools and districts. Chapter 9 closes part 2 and outlines the accelerating phase of deep change, highlighting short-cycle feedback and the measurement and celebration of meaningful progress.

In part 3, we consider the path ahead. In chapter 10, we consider how effective change leaders, rather than take pride in the execution of the plan, take pride in the many midcourse corrections that are required to recognize and respond to changing environmental realities. Moreover, they disseminate change plans in such a clear and practical manner that everyone in the organization can understand and own the elements of the plan. And, as we explore in chapter 11, effective change leaders anticipate the mistakes change leaders make—being an overly enthusiastic cheerleader, a schoolmaster for whom the rationale for change is self-evident, or a cynic who engages in superficial engagement in change but maintains subterranean resistance.

Finally, we close part 3 with chapter 12, in which we consider how to build a team of change leaders. Even when every other element of a change effort has been effective, the sustainability of the change is doomed when it is associated with a personality rather than an idea. Changes that have endured throughout history were certainly advanced by powerful personalities, but the ideas have been sustained not because of the personalities involved but because of the power of the ideas themselves: the primacy of mathematics on the African continent, Arabian Gulf, and central Asia; the foundations of liberty expressed in the Magna Carta; the elevation of reason over superstition in the Enlightenment; the supremacy of personal understanding over hierarch in the Reformation; and the revolutions on both sides of the Atlantic and in North and South America. To put a fine point on it, change leaders do not need to be Pythagoras, Luther, Bolívar, or Jefferson. They could be the other unheralded and unknown originators of algebra or the rights of humankind. Personalities dissipate. Ideas survive. Teams of change leaders will not say that they were inspired only by a person, however inspirational that person may have been. If the change endures, the team of change leaders will continue that effort because of the power of the idea that inspired them.

Each of the twelve research-based chapters features a reflection section at its close, in which prompts and queries serve to guide individuals, and ultimately schools and districts, through the intensive process of deep change.

Along the way, we will consider some contrary notions, including those posited by Leonard Mlodinow (2018), such as neophilia—love of change. From an evolutionary standpoint, Mlodinow (2018) suggests that contrary to the much-discussed resistance to change and fear of change, since prehistoric times, people have craved change. Indeed, it is change that led to our survival as a species. Without changes in location, diet, and activities, our species would not have survived. We are the weakest primates and most vulnerable to many predators, yet our ability to change and adapt to changing environments allowed our survival not of the *fittest* but of the most able to change. It is as if people and the organizations they create have two competing drives. While organizations often see the key to survival as static resistance to change, the people who created them know intuitively that survival requires change and adaptation. It is these competing narratives on which deep change leadership is based.

A BRIEF WORD ABOUT TERMINOLOGY

Authors sometimes take simple ideas and make them complicated. I aspire to the opposite. Over the last half of the 20th century and well into the 21st, academics have labored over the distinction between leaders and managers, as if a leader can be competent without superior management skills, and as if a manager can execute but lacks the vision to be a true leader. This book is for change leaders and those who aspire to lead deep change within their schools and educational systems. When I say *change leaders,* I mean those who understand that they require both leadership vision and the execution and planning skills associated with great management, expanding beyond the superficial boundaries between managers and leaders and entering the territory that matters most. Change leaders understand the necessity of vision and mission and also master the skills of management of time, projects, and people. Change leaders are not subservient to the traditions of strategic planning, with five-to-seven-year time horizons, but are capable of leading change at an accelerated pace to meet the urgent needs of their students. Change leaders are masters not of rhetoric but of reality—the day-to-day work that makes change happen. Change leaders inspire not with words but with actions.

PART 1

THE DEEP CHANGE IMPERATIVE

This book is about deep change—individual, team, organizational, and societal change. How is deep change distinct from the more-common superficial change? Whereas superficial change happens when posters featuring change slogans adorn the walls of schools and conference rooms, deep change influences our daily lives as educational professionals and, most important, the lives of our students. Superficial change has to do with format—such as delivering a lecture with a PowerPoint rather than a chalkboard. Deep change fundamentally alters the interactions between student and teacher, questioning the very premise on which the lecture tradition is based. Superficial change is about changing meeting protocols, while deep change involves changing the fundamental purpose and even the existence of the meeting. Superficial change is easy but unrewarding. Because it doesn't lead to action, superficial change breeds cynicism and contempt among busy faculty and staff members. Deep change is hard, but it is deeply rewarding because hardworking professionals can see the results of their work. Superficial change is about compliance. Deep change is about commitment.

Deep change bears a cost in personal, emotional, and psychic terms. It's about change that can be difficult and painful, in the way that muscles change only after they are exercised to the point of exhaustion. Muscles that are changed for the better first have microtears, suffering physical damage, and only then are renewed and strengthened. This is the sort of deep change on which the lives of individuals and organizations depend. It is difficult, unpopular, and painful.

This book is about changing not only ourselves and our organizations but also our neighborhoods and communities. It is about comparing what is to what could be and asking, as George Bernard Shaw, Robert Kennedy, and change agents throughout history famously asked, "Why not?" Many teachers from ancient to modern times devote their lives to finding evidence in support of previously conceived conclusions. That is why, even in the enlightened 21st century, more than 90 percent of hypotheses in academic journals are confirmed, according to researchers Ana Mlinarić, Martina Horvat, and Vesna Šupak Smolčić (2017). Such writers are no better than the fourth grader who, having mixed baking soda and vinegar, is astonished, bewildered, and truly amazed at the ensuing volcanic eruption. If you already know the results, then the project, however interesting, cannot be called experimental research.

Our guides in the following pages are not those who elevate certitude over facts but rather those who can admit when they were wrong. We cannot seek to change friends, families, teams, organizations, and societies if we lack evidence that we can change and have changed ourselves.

Chapter 1

Recognizing Schools' Need for Deep Change

Alarming warnings about the failures of the education systems in the United States and many other countries are not new. Jack Schneider (2018), assistant professor of leadership in education, recalls the rhetoric of alarm that began with the National Commission on Excellence in Education's (1983) *A Nation at Risk* and that continues decades after the report's publication. Students of history know that the Reagan administration was hardly original in its critique of public education. Author and educational consultant Matthew Lynch (2016) reminds us that the emphasis from the 1960s forward for a federal role in education in fact mirrored that of the 19th century. During that time, states became much more involved in education, which, in the early days of the United States had been almost entirely the concern of the villages, towns, and cities where students attended schools. Horace Mann's vision of the common school with public funding was based on the conviction that access to education was a right and that universal education would be attained only with state assistance (Lynch, 2016). It is therefore reasonable to ask, "After a couple of centuries of demanding change in public schools, why do these institutions remain so difficult to change?"

Schools are human institutions, and despite all the progress that humanity has made, strong forces militate against significant change and show a preference for superficial change. There are two factors required for change. The first is an individual decision to reject the past—accept the loss of previous practices and the comfort associated with them—and the willingness to try something new. The second is the organizational context that requires what Harvard Business School professor Amy C. Edmondson (2019) calls *psychological safety*. No matter how willing to change individuals might be, they are paralyzed in an environment in which the very discussion of change would require an admission of error. When individuals and organizations cannot talk about mistakes, Edmondson (2019) argues, learning is impossible. In Edmondson's (2019) research, psychological safety is not about being comfortable but rather about engaging in the discomfort of learning without fear. Learning—from learning to read to learning to lead—is hard work. If there is not an element of discomfort, of replacing old habits with new ones, then it is unlikely that learning is taking place. That was true in the days of Horace Mann in the 19th century and remains so in the 21st century. Based on more than two decades of research in medicine, business, nonprofit, education, and government organizations, Edmondson (2019) suggests that only about 20 percent of organizations have the levels of psychological safety sufficient to engage in serious change. The psychologically safe organization is one in which people observe data—from medical errors to low scores on reading and mathematics tests—and view the data not as accusations of incompetence but as invitations to inquiry. Despite the ready availability of data in so many classrooms, it remains common for the data that would be most revealing for teachers and leaders—that is, classroom-by-classroom data analysis—to be obscured through a focus on data for an entire grade level or school. The most common response I hear when I ask why we cannot examine classroom data is, "That would feel evaluative." Those words are clear evidence of a psychologically unsafe environment.

Leaders often blame the failure of change efforts on resisters—the people who approach change with fear and loathing and who are deeply committed to the comfort of present practice. Human resistance to change can be overwhelming, even in the face of evidence that demands change. Deutschman (2007), in the subtly titled book *Change or Die*, provides a compelling example of just how epic individual resistance to change can be. There is more than a half century of medical evidence on the ways to prevent and recover from coronary artery disease. Researchers estimate that the vast majority of risk factors are not genetic but rather the result of specific behavioral choices—smoking, drinking, insufficient exercise, poor diet, and so forth (Deutschman, 2007). That was true during the dawn of surgical interventions for coronary disease in the 1950s, and it remains true well into the 21st century. Perhaps patients from the 1950s could be excused for their habits—after all, a substantial number of physicians smoked, were overweight, and engaged in other unhealthy behaviors. So maybe it is not surprising that, even in the face of a potentially fatal heart attack, the behavior modification rate in the 1950s was less than 10 percent (Deutschman, 2007). But in the 21st century, with all the evidence and advanced medical knowledge we have and with all the public health information that cardiac care patients have received most of their adult lives, the patient response rate is not better; it has barely budged. Even with more than $60 billion spent annually on heart surgery and angioplasty, and an unquantifiable cost in pain and suffering for patients and their families, the behavior modification rate remains nearly at the same level as in the 1950s (Deutschman, 2007). In brief, when doctors tell patients, "Change or die," patients often make the latter choice. The same is true in schools. Although there is, for example, a clear consensus among educational researchers on the most effective ways to teach reading to students, English economist Tim Harford (2016) concludes that it is not a matter of ignorance of the scientific research but active resistance to it. Similarly, my research (Reeves, 2020a) on feedback and grading reveals that simple improvements in grading practices can reduce failure by dramatic margins, yet the fear of change is often greater than the fear of the lifelong consequences of school failure. When effective practices in the basics of reading instruction and effective feedback are denied to students, there is little outrage. Schools will often pursue, at great expense in time and money, just the right strategic plan, accompanied by speeches that accomplish little, while student failure continues to mount.

It is essential to note that resistance to change is not a character flaw. The reading teacher who sincerely believes that the scientific evidence on reading instruction is wrong is not evil. Rather, the teachers I've interviewed have made compelling observations—based on interactions with their own children—that suggest to them they can foster reading proficiency without the methods that the evidence supports (such as explicit phonics instruction). Similarly, the teachers who resist improvements in grading and feedback sincerely believe that their use of punitive grading policies is not pernicious but rather a deliberate and necessary strategy to prepare students for the real world.

It is not just the individual resistance to change that is the problem. Without psychological safety in a school or district, people will not talk about mistakes and learn from errors. Like the heart surgeons whose advice patients do not heed, Edmondson (2019) finds change efforts that were literally matters of life and death. When the traditions of strict hierarchy and very limited employee voice in South African mines, for example, made the miners and middle managers reluctant to talk about the cause of deaths and injuries of miners, individual and organizational learning was impossible, and the tragic toll continued. Fortunately, this dire situation could be improved, but it required the organization to provide an environment of psychological safety before it could successfully provide an environment of physical safety, and it required individual courage by leaders and employees to abandon the hierarchical models of intimidating leadership that had been part of the culture for decades. Similarly, there are schools that have, within a single year, dramatically improved reading instruction, transformed feedback and grading systems, and improved collaboration among faculty and administrators as they have elevated students' needs over the comforts of past practice. In sum, deep change is possible, whether in the hospital operating room, the first-grade classroom, or the high school mathematics department.

The problem is that most change literature focuses on factors such as individual willpower, a notoriously unreliable characteristic, rather than the collaborative efforts of the professionals involved in implementing the change. To attempt to make changes in the professional practices of individual teachers and administrators without first addressing the institutional, professional, and psychological support for a safe environment is an exercise in futility.

Despite these challenges, a growing body of evidence suggests that long-term sustainable change is possible. Professors Richard E. Boyatzis, Melvin Smith, and Ellen Van Oosten (2019) of Case Western Reserve University assemble more than three dozen studies that show not only that change is possible but that it can be effectively sustained over the course of five or more years. These researchers distinguish between change focused on compliance and change focused on compassion. While the former is often associated with avoiding something bad, the latter is aspirational. Compliance is associated with what we do—avoiding unwanted behaviors—while compassion is associated with who we want to be as people. The compelling evidence that Boyatzis and colleagues (2019) provide includes some of the situations most impervious to change, from hardened organizational practices to heroin addiction. They make the case that deep change can occur and has occurred, but rarely as a result of individual willpower or the brute force of compliance. Rather, their many examples of long-term sustained change feature consistent elements, including the collaborative professional and social support on which effective change depends.

To gain a better sense of this essential collaborative professional and social support, let's consider the difference between skeptics and cynics, reflect on the history of change leadership, and recognize the urgency of planning with purposeful action.

SKEPTICS AND CYNICS: DEALING WITH DEEP RESISTANCE TO CHANGE

Just as the right plan or workshop will not lead to change, neither will even the most effective collaborative and psychologically safe environment. There are instances in which resistance to change is so ingrained that it has nothing to do with policy and practice and everything to do with personal identity. If, for example, my identity as an educator is to have the opportunity every day to demonstrate my mastery of and even love for the subjects I teach, it can feel like an assault on that identity when I am told to allow students to engage in inquiry and struggle rather than dutifully take notes on my lectures. If, as an administrator, my identity is based on my ability to maintain a safe and orderly environment—something for which I have been praised by faculty, parents, and students—then my identity is challenged when new policies seek to keep in school rather than suspend those students with discipline problems. Most teachers and administrators who have been in the profession for a long time have seen a number of change programs come and go and thus are understandably skeptical of the latest enthusiasm of the day.

It is important, therefore, for change leaders to distinguish skeptics from cynics. Skeptics have reasonable grounds—logically and emotionally—to question new change initiatives. The most effective response to skeptics is not to bulldoze them but to engage them as partners in the process of inquiry. In the fall of 2020, for example, teachers in Marion, Ohio, were able to receive feedback within the first eight weeks of the school year that their new literacy program was having measurable and profound effects on student performance in reading (Walker, 2020). In San Bernardino City Unified School District in California in 2019, teachers and administrators reported to me that high school mathematics and science teachers could see a decrease in the failure rate by more than 80 percent, reducing sections of students repeating required classes, and improving behavior, attendance, and classroom culture—all in one semester. In Cardinal, Iowa, in one year, simple changes in homework policies led to a reduction in the failure rate of more than 90 percent and a reduction in suspensions of 55 percent. What these examples of change efforts have in common is the process of inquiry accompanied by clear and measurable impact—after which the buy-in came (we'll explore buy-in in greater depth in chapter 3, page 37).

But what if, even after compelling evidence of success, we have educators and administrators who persist in resisting change? That is the action not of a skeptic, who is guided by evidence, but of a cynic, who cares more about personal preference than evidence. Educational leaders are not helpless when confronting cynics. A teacher once told me that the "value of autonomy" was paramount. "Even more than the value of student learning?" I asked. The reply was emphatically in the affirmative. Deep change will be most likely to occur when skeptics change practice, notice the benefits, and make resistance to the change more uncomfortable than acceptance of it. Nevertheless, there will always come a time when leaders have to take decisive action, however unpopular, to serve the needs of students.

HOW WE GOT HERE: A BRIEF HISTORY OF CHANGE LEADERSHIP

Change leadership has traditionally been the result of both scholars' intellectual leadership and the translation of that intellectual leadership into leadership and professional practices. Two scholars who exemplify intellectual leadership that has led to changes in teaching and leadership are Harvard professors Howard Gardner and John Kotter. For more than a half century, Howard Gardner (1999, 2007) upended traditional notions of intelligence by propounding the theory of multiple intelligences, that intelligence is not merely reflected in traditional tests of verbal and mathematical ability, the tests that have dominated the field since the early 20th century. A few blocks away from Gardner's office at the Harvard Graduate School of Education, John Kotter teaches leadership classes at the Harvard Business School. Kotter's (1995; Kotter & Cohen, 2012) writings on organizational change have dominated the field since the 1980s and influenced two generations of leaders in business, government, nonprofit, and education. However different their academic disciplines, Gardner and Kotter have one remarkable trait in common: they both have described, publicly and clearly, how well-intentioned leaders and practitioners have badly applied their theories. In a joint appearance we made in a Boston-area public library, Gardner and I talked about our research and writing. He was modest and self-effacing, stating emphatically that he had propounded theories to be tested and not provided definitive conclusions to be followed. He was dismayed by those who, for example, claimed to have "multiple-intelligences schools," as if he had published scientifically conclusive results rather than theories designed to be submitted to the community of scholars for testing and challenge. Though Kotter is widely known for his eight-stage model of change, one of his least-referenced articles is titled "Leading Change: Why Transformation Efforts Fail" (Kotter, 1995). Michael Fullan (2008, 2011, 2019) has a global reputation as a leading theorist on change in educational systems, but he acknowledges how the field of change theory has, well, changed. When people challenge him about his often-quoted contention that systemic change requires a half decade or more, Fullan responds, "I've learned a few things about change in the past forty years, and that includes accelerating the pace of change" (M. Fullan, personal communication, December 6, 2017).

Those who write about change leadership in the 21st century would benefit from the modest models Gardner, Kotter, and Fullan offer. Strategic plans and organizational-leadership presentations are dominated by phrases such as *theory of action*, without a hint that all theories must be tested and are often found wanting. Leaders who propound theories of action must always ask, "How will we know if we are right or wrong?" Indeed, the acid test of authenticity for leaders and researchers is the candid acknowledgment of our errors and our willingness to learn from those mistakes and help others to do the same.

Change theory from the 1980s has dominated the field well into the 21st century. These theories have been fatally flawed by the claim writer Brianna Wiest (2016) articulates that to change our lives we must change our minds. This model of thinking our way into change is the foundation of endless series of change rallies in which leaders desperately seek buy-in for their latest vision of change.

The foundation of the multibillion-dollar training industry for corporations, government entities, nonprofits, and educational organizations is that with just the right combination of training through keynotes, workshops, and online courses, employees will change their attitudes and beliefs and, as a result, change their actions. But as Johns Hopkins University researcher Robert Slavin (2019) argues, there is scant evidence to support this supposition. Michael Beer, Magnus Finnström, and Derek Schrader (2016) report in the *Harvard Business Review* that corporate leadership training programs are similarly ineffective. Perhaps the change technique with the worst combination of high cost and little impact is the practice of attempting to evaluate people into better performance. Authors Marcus Buckingham and Ashley Goodall (2019), in the aptly titled *Nine Lies About Work*, show that there is not a scintilla of evidence that demonstrates that corporate evaluation programs are reliable (that is, consistent) or valid (that is, that they measure what they purport to measure). The elusive idea of measuring employee "potential" is what Buckingham and Goodall (2019) find particularly objectionable, as the term is nearly mystical in its imprecision. The worst examples of evaluation come from the field of education, where, since the turn of the century, state legislatures and school districts have fallen under the thrall of "value-added evaluation" in which, as a result of a complex statistical formula, the system claims to be able to identify which teachers add value to student learning and which do not. The problem is, as Valerie Strauss (2012) reports, it doesn't work. There are practical issues as well. If an evaluation system is to motivate employees, then those employees must understand the system and the rationale behind the evaluation. To be effective as a lever for change, the employees and their managers must see a clear path toward improvement. But contemporary evaluation systems—and especially the value-added systems—do not do that. Their complexity and opaque nature leave employees with unhelpful answers to, "What do I need to do to improve?" such as, "Well, everybody gets a 3," "I just don't give out 5s," "It's a very complicated formula; you wouldn't understand it," and, my favorite, "The formula is proprietary intellectual property, so we can't disclose it." Most evaluation systems are worse than no evaluation at all because they are counterproductive, demoralizing employees and leaving them with a sense of hopelessness and futility that undermines performance and morale. The final issue for complex evaluation systems is that they are inconsistent. Imagine that you step on the scale and it reads 150 pounds. You do the same tomorrow, and it reads 100 pounds. The next day, the scale reads 200 pounds. Would you believe that your weight was really changing by that degree every day, or would you believe that the scale was broken? If the latter response is obvious, then it's clear why evaluation scales, such as the value-added system, are so deeply broken. This year's A teacher is next year's F teacher and the following year's B teacher. In sum, mystery does not motivate.

FROM PLANS TO ACTION

Ineffective change efforts are often characterized by the twin perils of complexity and rhetoric, with the first characterized by impenetrable jargon and the second by facile slogans. Jeffrey Pfeffer (2015), in the brilliant book *Leadership BS,* notes that inspiration is not sufficient to create change. Too many leaders and certainly, he argues, too many universities seek only to inspire without the foundation of evidence and facts on which sustainable inspiration must be based. People neither need nor benefit from fables about heroic leaders making gut-level decisions that, as if propelled by miraculous forces, turn out to be just right.

It is not that traditional planning is without value; nimble planning is essential for any effective school or district. In fact, strategic planning is so important that it should not be left exclusively in the hands of strategic planners; nor should the evidence of the impact of strategic planning be restricted to production of a strategic plan. The document itself does not fully reflect the value of the process; that lies in the communication, the linkages, and the focus provided by the process of collaborative data analysis and goal setting. Most strategic-planning processes, says Spark (n.d.), confirm existing mental models by starting with a statement of belief systems that yield some typically expected statement, such as "People are our greatest asset" or "All people can learn and grow," sometimes boldly modified to be "All people will learn and grow." The missing conversation, however, is the confrontation of the chasm between these statements and the reality of schools and districts, policies, and other operational evidence of belief systems. The process of articulating values and belief systems is one thing; the process of listing the values and beliefs that are reflected in the daily lives of schools and districts is quite another. Unless we are willing to say that beliefs have fundamentally changed, we should not expect strategic planning, no matter how elaborate the process, how large the document, or how pretentious the vocabulary, to yield meaningful improvement. Change can occur, however. Schools, districts, and educators can engage in effective change not as a result of documents but as a result of the application of a change model that rests on a vivid vision, clear results, short-term wins, and shared responsibility. Change under any circumstances is not popular, but the goal in the following pages is not popularity but positive impact. Even when the need for change is overwhelming, change leaders will encounter resistance to change from both skeptics and cynics. And planning without action—decisive, immediate, focused, and accelerated action—is a prescription for frustration.

CONCLUSION

Whenever people claim that change is easy, they are simply not asking for anything but the most superficial change. The challenges of change are hardly unique to the 21st century. Decades of research and theory have propounded different mechanisms for personal and organizational change, and despite this avalanchc of advice, individuals who face pain and death for failure to change remain remarkably impervious to making the essential changes. Business, nonprofits, and educational organizations also cling to past practice, even as they confront bankruptcy; extinction; and an exodus of customers, clients, and students. The most common mechanism for change, the five-year strategic plan (and many organizations engage in the fantasy of ten-, twenty-, and fifty-year plans), is yet another piece of expensive and time-consuming consulting advice that belongs on the scrap heap of history. As a result of these failed mechanisms for change, there is little wonder that leaders face skeptics and cynics whenever they suggest innovative ideas. However, there must be a careful distinction between these potential opponents to change initiatives. Skeptics, having been through several failed change ideas, have a good reason for their skepticism. They want to see evidence that the new idea will have a chance of success, and they want more than the enthusiasm and vague promises of leaders. They want progress reports and evidence that their efforts are working, and, most of all, they want to know how they contribute to the accomplishment of educational goals. They need a sense of purpose and meaning that links their actions and those of their colleagues to observable results. If they were involved in what is notoriously the most difficult of change efforts—weight loss—they might not expect to see results in a week, but they certainly would expect to see results within one hundred days, or they would not sustain their regimen of diet and exercise. The same is true with instructional and leadership techniques. We can and must accelerate the pace of change and measure both implementation and results in the short term.

Despite this legacy of failed change efforts, however, there is hope for the future. Significant and transformational change has happened in business, nonprofit, and educational organizations, and we can learn from their common elements. In the chapters ahead, we will meet educators and leaders who engaged in deep change that provided immediate and profound results for students, improved morale for staff, and brought about long-term benefits for the communities that they serve.

REFLECTION

Review the following prompts, and record your responses someplace where you can easily refer to them throughout the deep change journey.

1. Describe the most successful personal change effort you have observed. Perhaps it was a change you made, or that of a family member or friend. What prompted the change? What support did the person making the change receive? How did the person know he or she was successful? If the change had not been made, what would the consequences have been?
2. Describe the most successful school change you have observed; it may have been in a single classroom, among a group of colleagues, or within an entire school or system. What prompted the change?

What support did the team making the change receive? How did the team members know that they were successful? If the change had not been made, what would the consequences have been?

3. Reflect on a failed change effort. Why was the change not successful?

Chapter 2

Understanding the Pain Inherent in Change

In this chapter, we will consider the pain of change. However beneficial a prospective change might be for an individual or a school, change means the loss of past practice. It means acknowledging that what we were doing in the past was not as effective as what we might do in the future. Whether the change is that we are helping a student learn to play the violin, preparing ourselves for a marathon, or familiarizing ourselves with a new technology program for the classroom, there is a common theme to these efforts. The process of change can be frustrating and painful. People have meltdowns not merely over major changes, such as organizational restructuring or relocations, but also over what might seem trivial—the movement of a desk from one part of the floor to another; a change in classrooms; a change in meeting format; or changes in software, calendars, and operational systems. Resistance to change is not necessarily a function of organizational size or complexity. The U.S. military, an organization characterized by giant size, enormous complexity, and long-standing tradition, has engaged in remarkable transformations in training, leadership, logistics, and acquisition, much of it driven by the need to respond immediately to the threats to the country and allies in the aftermath of the September 11, 2001, terrorist attacks (Gouré, 2018). I have also seen small schools and districts struggle with relatively minor changes. Whatever the scale or complexity, change is difficult and painful and will almost always meet resistance. In this chapter, we will begin by considering why change is painful—psychologically and physically—and the root of resistance to change. We'll also work out why even the most obviously beneficial changes, changes that have zero pain and great benefits, are nevertheless met with resistance. Finally, we'll explore the joy of change.

WHY CHANGE IS PAINFUL

Some changes cause physical pain. For example, fasting can cause stomach cramps; effective exercise routines create microtears in the muscles that grow in strength after a series of tears, recoveries, and repetitions; and running, particularly long distances, can cause pain in the hips, knees, and feet. There are no surprises here. But what about the changes that happen in organizations? It turns out that the pain that change inflicts on people is not merely inconvenience but psychological and even physical pain, according to researchers Jane E. Dutton and Gretchen M. Spreitzer (2014). Dutton and Spreitzer (2014) suggest that when leading change, we must use one of the strategies employed by people recovering from injury, surgery, and serious diseases: mindfulness. They argue that a key leadership characteristic is compassion, understanding the pain of colleagues undergoing change in the same way that we would be compassionate about a colleague who is sick or suffering a serious loss. We extend compassion naturally to those who are in pain and burdened by suffering. Change leaders deliberately seek to understand the pain that is truly present for those undergoing change. While Boyatzis and colleagues (2019) find that it is possible to have people embrace change, that transformation happens only in the presence of compassion. Without it, would-be change leaders gain only sullen short-term compliance, not long-term sustainable change.

One of the best examples of transformative change has been the widespread implementation of the Professional Learning Community (PLC) at Work® process. Anyone lucky enough to have heard the testimony of the late Richard DuFour would have no doubt about the wisdom and efficacy of his ideas. At least, of course, until they implemented those practices. While the collaborative practices of Richard DuFour, Rebecca DuFour, Robert Eaker, Thomas W. Many, and Mike Mattos (2016) have had demonstrable success in schools around the world, the implementation is challenging. For a teacher used to taking enormous pride in creating the lessons and assessments for a class, the use of collaborative teams to create common lessons and assessments meant not only a loss of personal time spent in solitary preparation but also the loss of autonomy. Those used to being the sole arbiters of what student work was excellent, mediocre, or unacceptable suddenly had other people—sometimes faculty members junior to them—looking over their shoulders. I've been in these meetings, where there were anger and tears. Change, especially in the presence of others, is difficult and painful.

Changes in educational leadership can be similarly painful, with a superintendent or building principal dominating traditional cabinet meetings and faculty meetings, while the cabinet or faculty provides an audience. That model remains dominant in many schools I visit. But leaders intent on deep change get off the stage, just as they ask classroom educators to do, and turn these meetings into professional learning opportunities. But if I have spent a quarter century reaching this position of leadership, it's not easy to give up the trappings of authority.

THE ROOT OF RESISTANCE TO CHANGE

Physical and emotional change are not the only reasons that people resist change. Demands for change at work, and even well-intentioned suggestions from loved ones, rarely sound like supportive, positive messages. The words may be "Honey, you'd look great in these pants!" but the message we hear is "I must look terrible in the pants I'm wearing." The supervisor who intends to be encouraging and supportive says, "You're going to really enjoy this professional learning program for student engagement," but the teacher hears, "My principal must think I'm a terrible teacher who doesn't engage students." Major change efforts expand the opportunities for catastrophic thinking. Within hours of hearing that a superintendent is retiring, administrators in the district have called me wondering whether they should start looking for a new job. No one suggested that their jobs were in jeopardy, and some had recently received perfect performance reviews—the highest-possible ratings. Yet they were convinced nevertheless that a change in senior leadership meant that other senior leaders faced potential termination. This visceral fear is similar to what one feels when suddenly plunged into darkness, without any clear marker to find one's way. It is jarring and, ultimately, terrifying. Consider the change that kids make from walking, a skill they have mastered since toddlerhood, to riding a bicycle. Try to remember the first time you attempted to ride a bicycle without training wheels. Perhaps at first there were the reassuring hands of a parent or older sibling on the back of the seat. You knew that you would not fall. But ultimately these guiding hands let go, and after sailing away happily for a few feet, you realized that you could not steer. The encounter with a curb, the pavement, or, in my case, a parked car was abrupt and painful. Thus, the association of change with pain begins early in life and is part of our lifetime understanding of the impact of change in our lives. It is not impossible to overcome the pain of change—babies learn to walk, kids learn to ride bicycles, and middle-aged out-of-shape nonathletes run marathons. Moribund organizations can be transformed, creating new opportunities for employees and customers. Institutions with ancient roots, from universities to symphony orchestras to national and state governments, can change and have changed. But it is simply not without pain and resistance.

The root of resistance to change is that even when we want to change, we are confronting the fact that we are not acceptable as we are. Though this confrontation need not be as catastrophic as we imagine, it certainly feels that way. I need to learn more—something I find exciting—but if I don't, then my brain will atrophy, I will lose value to my colleagues and clients, and I will disengage from the world. I need to maintain my health, something that I rationally understand, but if I fail to do everything exactly right, my health will suffer anyway, so why put forth the effort? In other words, we sometimes exaggerate the impact of our failure to change, facing the deep humiliation of just how unacceptable we are. Change leaders ignore this psychological principle at their peril: change, no matter how well intended and well communicated, tells the people you are asking to change that they are not acceptable as they are, and that really hurts.

Rosabeth Moss Kanter (2012) reminds us that the resistance to change that people express is not associated with the present change alone but rather a reflection of every change—successful and unsuccessful—that they have endured. No matter how well executed the current change effort may be, the people responsible for implementing it are operating under the shadow of previous changes that might have included excessive demands, job loss, insecurity, and feelings of incompetence. We are all the sum of our histories, and effective change leaders will take the time to learn about past experiences with change and invite the entire team to contribute to learning from the mistakes of the past.

WHY EVEN OBVIOUSLY BENEFICIAL CHANGE HURTS

Harvard professor Robert Kegan and lecturer Lisa Laskow Lahey (2009) argue that even people who, on the surface, profess to want to embrace change often have hidden alternative commitments that compete for their attention and focus. They use the term *immunity to change* to describe this quandary and compare resistance to change to how the body's immune system isolates and kills foreign bacteria (Kegan & Lahey, 2009). The path beyond immunity to change is the identification and exposure of these competing commitments, which are not obvious. This phenomenon happens when people listen to the leader's case for change, enthusiastically agree with it, participate actively in any new training required, incorporate the change plans into their personal and professional goals and objectives, and then do absolutely nothing to implement the change. This is enormously frustrating for leaders, who much assume that these people are just classic change resisters and will never engage in the meaningful change that the organization needs. But, Kegan and Lahey (2009) suggest, they are often unaware of their competing commitments.

Among the greatest competing commitments when faced with the need for change is a fear of incompetence. The sense of being good at what we do is an important part of personal identity and emotional security, starting at a very early age. "Every child is an artist," Picasso said. "The problem is how to remain an artist once he grows up" (Modern Living, 1976).

Five-year-olds will gleefully experiment with singing, dancing, painting, and writing poetry. But soon the need for perfection exceeds the willingness to take risks and try new skills. By early adolescence, a student might say, "I'm great at mathematics, but I'm just not a good writer," or vice versa. "I love video games, but I hate reading," another will say. There is very rarely a cognitive impairment that would stop students from learning all these skills, but according to psychotherapist Michael Borg-Laufs (2013), their greatest need—and one that increases as they grow older—is the need to be competent in front of their friends and colleagues. Students will sit quietly in class, and administrators will do the same in meetings, not asking questions because they fear that posing a question would expose what they do not know. Change leaders understand this fundamental need for competence and confidence and thus avoid establishing change efforts as a chaotic set of demands that elevate the uncertainty and self-doubt associated with anything new or different. Although one level of the hierarchy often assumes that only those at lower levels are responsible for resistance to change, the truth is that emotional contagion extends from the top and can infect every layer of an organization (Schwartz, 2012). Even when the leader makes heartfelt pleas for change, subordinates can perceive fear and uncertainty. A litany of management buzzwords over the years, such as *re-engineering, rightsizing,* and *optimizing,* may have been trotted out with Ivy League sophistication and lots of enthusiasm, but what people want to know is, "Does this mean I'm going to lose my job?" It's difficult to embrace change when fear and preoccupation over meeting basic needs of food and shelter may be on the line. For children and adolescents in particular, according to researchers Annina Riggenbach, Liesbet Goubert, Stijn

Van Petegem, and Rémy Amouroux (2019), this fear-avoidance mechanism is a primary coping skill—and the need to embrace certainty and avoid fear does not evaporate in adulthood.

It's easy to see how gripping the fear of incompetence and insecurity can be, and likewise, it's understandable why people might resist beneficial changes like giving up cigarettes and martinis, as withdrawal from addictive substances can be enormously painful. But what about a change that offered enormous benefits to you and your schools, had seemingly zero cost and zero pain, and provided an impressive combination of financial rewards and personal recognition? Surely in such a situation, competing commitments wouldn't figure into the equation and resistance to change would evaporate? If you think so, consider the "granny shot" in which a basketball player stands at the free-throw line and, rather than shooting at the basket in the typical overhand way, launches the ball underhanded. Because it is a free throw, there is no danger of the ball being stolen by a defensive player. All the basketball player needs to do is just put his or her hands on the sides of the basketball and throw it. The evidence in favor of the granny shot is incontrovertible: author Mayo Oshin (2018) writes that players who use this technique hit a higher percentage of their free throws than those who do not. Basketball greats Rick Barry, who introduced the technique, and Wilt Chamberlain used this shot to great effect in winning championships. Because many games are decided by razor-thin margins, any slight edge that might increase one's free-throw percent from, say, 50 percent to 60 percent could represent the difference between winning and losing games and championships. When Chamberlain used this technique, his percentage of successful shots more than doubled, from 40 percent to 87 percent. But for reasons we can only speculate on, Barry continued to use the shot, and Chamberlain abandoned it. In 2020, there are two players in the NBA who use this technique—Rick Barry's son, Canyon Barry, and Chinanu Onuaku. In this league where millions of dollars, lifetime financial security, and the adulation of fans depend on scoring points, players from Wilt Chamberlain to the present would apparently rather avoid looking silly, as the granny shot perhaps makes them feel, and forgo money and points. While teachers and school administrators do not, alas, reap the financial rewards of professional athletes, they do gain recognition and personal satisfaction when their students succeed. Very simple changes in grading practices, such as eliminating the average and using a four-point scale (in which A is 4, B is 3, C is 2, and D and F are 1) rather than a one-hundred-point scale, are linked to immediate and profound improvement in student results. Yet for reasons as mysterious as the resistance to the granny shot, most schools will not make these simple changes.

Psychologist Roy F. Baumeister and journalist John Tierney (2011) recommend that we practice small changes, such as brushing our teeth with our nondominant hands, taking different routes to work, and otherwise making small and relatively painless changes part of daily routines in order to systematically break down the inherent resistance to change that affects almost everyone. In schools, relatively small changes can help students and staff expand their comfort zones. For example, when teachers use equity sticks—that is, when they randomly call on students rather than wait for hands to be raised—it engages more students and prevents students from opting out of class. I've seen administrators do the same with staff meetings and collaborative team meetings in order to ensure that every voice is heard and that a few people do not dominate the discussion.

THE JOY IN CHANGE

Fortunately, it is possible that change can bring joy and fulfillment. Richard E. Boyatzis and colleagues (2019) offer some of the most encouraging news on change. Their extensive research over more than three decades on change suggests that leaders have two choices. They can coach for compliance—reinforcing every fear—or coach with compassion. Just as a focus on compliance can undermine change efforts, so too can an emphasis on *sympathy*. This patronizing perspective can be alluring, as many leaders are promoted as a result of their ability to both get things done and be seen by their subordinates as kind and understanding managers. But however attractive the sympathetic leader may appear, it paralyzes the team, says researcher Liz Wiseman (2017), maintaining the leader as the fixer and infantilizing the team. The leader is not only boss but parent, and that combination offers an exponential level of potential resentments. Empathy, by contrast, is born of compassion. The team members are not helpless but empowered adults with the ability to learn, make decisions, and accept or reject the opportunities before them.

In order to turn fear into hope, it is essential that change leaders engage the aspirations and dreams of their colleagues. That is why the change process that Boyatzis has pioneered invests time in personal vision statements. Often, adults are reluctant to share their dreams and visions, lest they seem to be engaged in trivial fantasizing when there is serious work to be done. But the key to unlocking the joy of change is recognizing that hopes and visions are never trivial.

Some of the best examples of transforming relatively small steps into public visions of success occur in a science fair–type setting, in which teachers and administrators showcase the results of their work in simple three-panel displays. All the displays follow the same format, with the left-hand column presenting the challenge, the middle column detailing the professional practice, and the right-hand column revealing the results. I have seen these displays in a variety of settings—collected from teachers within a single school and from teachers across an entire state—and the results are amazing. Teachers who thought that their small improvements in student literacy, behavior, or attendance were idiosyncratic find colleagues who have achieved similar results. What they thought was an isolated practice unworthy of replication could in fact comprise a set of evidence that drives deep change. Even with the most difficult challenges, such as policies in behavior and grading, this science fair approach helps propel change in a way that is faster and more effective than the publication of plans and policies. It is also the best way I know of to promote and celebrate teacher leadership with local models of effective practice that have an impact on student success.

The vast majority of people want not only to be successful but also to be seen as contributors to their teams, communities, and families. Moreover, precisely at a time when people can feel that their sense of worth and professional competence may be threatened by a change effort, it is especially important to reinforce their sense of autonomy and competence, which accompanies the many roles that they play in life. Leaders can promote this by creating profiles of staff that showcase not only their professional work inside the school but the many other roles that they play as family members, community leaders, social media stars, and so on. When change leaders replace fear with hope, there are immense psychological and performance benefits. As psychologist Hendrie Weisinger and performance coach J. P. Pawliw-Fry (2015) find, high levels of hope are associated with satisfaction, self-esteem, optimism, meaning in life, and happiness. Most relevant to this chapter is their finding that high levels of hope are associated with the ability to cope better with injuries, disease, and pain (Weisinger & Pawliw-Fry, 2015). Change leaders, in sum, don't avoid the pain of change but rather understand it, accept it, and give team members the necessary hope to deal successfully with pain.

CONCLUSION

There is real pain—physical and psychological—associated with change. Resistance to change is not, for the most part, the result of bad motives in which people deliberately disrespect leaders or their ideas. Rather, resistance to change has deep roots in early memories and the physical symptoms that we encounter when change, however desirable, has been painful. We equate the ecstasy of being given the new bicycle for our birthday with the pain of seeing both the bicycle and our knees get a few cuts and scrapes as we learned a new skill. With every change in technology, office arrangement, or even seating at a conference table, changes entail a range of reactions, almost all of them deeply uncomfortable. Even obviously advantageous changes meet resistance, and it takes a Chinanu Onuaku to show us that shedding the cultural fear of looking silly might be worth a few million dollars and league championships. The good news is that there is joy on the other side of pain, and the hope engendered by change leaders is the antidote to despair.

Though change leaders can inspire their teams and highlight the benefits of change, a significant barrier to change remains, and that is leaders' assumption that with just the right message, the right inspirational slogan, or the right sort of pep rally, every stakeholder will rally around the flag and buy into the proposed change. This presumption is based on the theory that changes in actions occur only after changes in the hearts and minds of employees. This is the destructive myth that we will explore in the next chapter.

REFLECTION

Review the following prompts, and record your responses someplace where you can easily refer to them throughout the deep change journey.

1. Describe a change—personal or professional—you implemented that resulted in success. It might have been enrollment in a challenging class in college, an interpersonal conflict that you resolved, or a shift in health habits. What parts of this change were most painful?
2. Describe a situation in which you felt completely in control—you were competent, in charge, and absolutely certain that you were not only doing the right thing but also doing it right, perhaps even perfectly. Hold that scene in your mind, and describe how it feels.
3. Review your responses to the previous two questions. How does the pain of change compare to the feeling of autonomy and control?
4. How can you help yourself and your colleagues gain greater feelings of autonomy and competence?
5. What are the greatest sources of fear right now for you and your colleagues? What can you do to counter fear and uncertainty with psychological safety?

Chapter 3

Exposing the Myth of Buy-In

There is a prevailing mythology of change leadership in which, if we just find the right blend of persuasion, research, and emotional appeal, staff will embrace the changes that leaders wish to make. This erroneous belief is based on the myth of buy-in—that in order to implement effective change, leaders must first gain widespread agreement from staff. When leaders tell me they have buy-in from all their staff members, one of two things is true: either (1) they are not really asking for significant change or, more likely, (2) the real resistance is happening underground, out of earshot of the leader. This is why the vast majority of change initiatives fail; remember from the introduction that, according to Kotter (2008), roughly 90 percent of change efforts are not implemented as intended.

As we explored in chapter 2 (page 27), change of any sort is difficult and painful. Change represents a loss—a loss of prior practices and a loss of an established comfort zone. Those who claim they can make change easy or popular have never led a significant change effort. In this chapter, I'm suggesting we toss aside the myth of buy-in and instead acknowledge the challenges and difficulties associated with change, treating our colleagues in a respectful manner even when they disagree with a proposed change. We must replace desperate appeals for agreement with a thoughtful, respectful, and reasoned approach to the uncertainty and difficulty that surround all change efforts. In the following pages, we'll consider how change leaders can adjust their mindsets to put behavior before belief, change the leadership conversation, avoid buy-in entirely when it comes to safety and values, and rethink positive thinking.

PUT BEHAVIOR BEFORE BELIEF

No more inspirational speeches. No more imperious demands. Just a considerate, respectful dialogue that goes something like this:

> *Our past change efforts have failed because leadership presented only the rosy predictions of success without transparently discussing the downside: the things that could go wrong, the costs in time and aggravation, and the lessons learned from other schools. So we're not going to repeat those mistakes. For every change idea, we will thoroughly consider both advantages and disadvantages, and we will have several alternative decisions, knowing that none of the possible decisions will be perfect.*

Harvard Law School lecturers Douglas Stone and Sheila Heen (2014) maintain that this open and transparent process for initiating change doesn't avoid opposition but rather engages opposition in an honest and thoughtful way. Consider these examples on some very sensitive topics that are difficult to change.

- **Teacher and administrator evaluation:** Since the publication of Charlotte Danielson and Thomas L. McGreal's (2000) *Teacher Evaluation to Enhance Professional Practice*, teacher evaluation using what is often referred to as the *Danielson rubric* has been pervasive in education around the world. The title of the book is telling, as it assumes that the purpose of evaluation is to "enhance professional practice." That is a testable hypothesis. If, after many years of schools using this evaluation tool, teacher professional practices demonstrably improved, then the claim in the book title would be validated. There are, however, significant challenges to this presumption. As researchers Rachel Garrett and Matthew P. Steinberg (2015) point out, the relationship between the ratings and teacher quality is circular. The evaluation does not cause teachers to get better; rather, the higher ratings are assigned to teachers who were already performing at a high level. Moreover, as writers Clayton M. Christensen, Michael B. Horn, and Curtis W. Johnson (2011) explain, merely putting words into a rubric format does not guarantee objectivity. Ambiguous language leads to inconsistent ratings, they note, and undermines the fundamental requirement of any assessment—reliability. Despite these limitations, the use of the Danielson rubric and other teacher evaluation tools remains widespread, and it hinges on the theory that teachers can be evaluated into better performance. That is inconsistent with my experience, in which I have seen many people coached into better performance, but I cannot recall a single instance of people being evaluated into better performance. Whereas coaching can be a collaborative enterprise in which the coach and the teacher work on goals supported by feedback, evaluation—in which one's job and financial security are on the line—is an adversarial process. Nevertheless, just as in the corporate world, school systems persist in their belief that evaluation improves performance.

- **Writing:** A substantial body of evidence (National Writing Project, 2009; Reeves, 2020a) concludes that when students write in every subject—not just English but mathematics; science; social studies; and even art, music, and physical education—there is a consistent and positive impact on every subject. When students write more—especially when the writing is focused on persuasion, comparison, evaluation, and other nonfiction modes of writing—their performance in all subjects improves. Despite this evidence, however, the opposition to cross-disciplinary writing is pervasive. Rather than plead for buy-in, here is a better way to have the conversation:

  We've all heard the research on the power of writing to improve student achievement, but I want you to know that I heard the skepticism very clearly. You're busy, and besides, most of you are not trained as teachers of writing. So I'm not asking you for buy-in right now. I'm just asking for a fair chance. You choose the day, you choose the prompt, and you choose how or whether to grade it. All I'm asking is that once each month for the next four months, you have a nonfiction writing prompt linked to your curriculum. Perhaps you will ask students to explain a graph in mathematics, describe a map in social studies, or describe an experiment in science. I'm asking that you use our very brief, simplified rubric—it's only about one-third of a page. We should all expect students to write coherently, spell correctly, and support their claims with evidence in every subject. You are the subject experts and can assess content however you wish. I promise that we'll then look at the results at the end of the semester and evaluate for ourselves whether the national research on writing is relevant to our school. To be clear, I know that many of you are skeptical, and I value and respect skeptics. Skeptics brought us the

Enlightenment. Skeptics brought us the Scientific Revolution. Skepticism is how we learn and grow. So it's OK to be skeptical—but let's give this a fair try and learn together what works best for our students in our school.

- **Grading reform:** There are few topics more controversial than the reform of grading practices. It is a global issue, with controversies over grading practices taking place on every continent. Opposition to even the simplest reforms has led to legislative opposition and the termination of leaders who dare to take on this highly emotional issue. But even with such a sensitive subject, there is a better way to approach change. Rather than implement an overhaul in grading systems that inevitably creates tension among faculty and parents, start small. I have seen very skeptical teachers make presentations to their colleagues about small changes in their grading systems. "I wasn't ready to change everything," said one California high school science teacher:

  > But I just changed two things—I stopped using the average to calculate semester grades, and I went back to our old-fashioned A, B, C, D, F grading scale, just like we calculate grade-point averages, with A = 4, B = 3, C = 2, D = 1, and F = 1. I got rid of the 100-point scale. That was it—just those two changes, and this semester, with the same curriculum and same assessments, I had more than 40 fewer Ds and Fs. It really made a difference. Students who used to fail were willing to show resilience, work hard, and achieve at higher levels. I also noticed that student behavior was significantly better because I didn't have students who had just emotionally checked out due to certain failure. (Reeves, 2010)

  I could have given a thousand speeches on grading that were not as effective as this one teacher speaking to his colleagues with evidence from students in his school.

In his book *Atomic Habits,* James Clear (2018) takes a powerful evidence-based approach to how individuals and organizations change. It is not through massive changes but through incremental improvements with measurable results. No bizarrely complicated strategic plans. No improvement plans that sit on the shelf. It's frequent actions—like writing just once a month or small improvements in grading practices that are widely accepted as reasonable and that can show results in a single semester. So let's drop the illusion of buy-in and just have respectful and evidence-based discussions with our colleagues.

CHANGE THE LEADERSHIP CONVERSATION

Consider two different leadership conversations. In the first, the leader begs, pleads, and cajoles. "Please, oh please, accept this change! Here is the evidence. Here is the reasoning. Please accept it!" This is unseemly and leads only to employees' cynicism. Employees have heard many pleas for change, all based on research, and watched as those change efforts floundered. The second conversation is quite different:

> *I want you to know that I respect our differences. We both are smart people and simply believe that the organization should go in different directions. So I'm not asking you for buy-in or agreement. Rather, I'm asking that you implement this plan to the best of your ability. If it fails, I will admit it in front of our entire team, and we'll see what we can learn from that failure. If it succeeds, we'll also discuss the lessons of success in front of our team. Either way, you and I will both learn from the experience. Will that work for you?*

Effective leaders do not need universal agreement, and if they think they have it, they are mistaken. What leaders do require is respect, not acquiescence. As historian Doris Kearns Goodwin (2005) brilliantly explains in her biography of Abraham Lincoln and his cabinet members in *Team of Rivals*, an effective group of people who have sufficient psychological safety can engage in the vigorous contest of ideas, challenging one another with vigor and respect. By appointing his rivals to his cabinet and innermost circle of advisers, Goodwin noted, Lincoln didn't give up authority but rather made some of the most critical decisions in the history of the republic when the nation was at its greatest peril. He made those decisions not from the gut or with sycophants giving him adoring affirmation but in the cauldron of debate and friction and starkly different alternatives. From that contentious environment grew decisions that saved the United States.

DON'T VOTE ON SAFETY AND VALUES

In an analysis I conducted of teacher perceptions of decision-making processes and actual decision-making practices (Reeves, 2020c), I found a striking disconnection between perceptions and reality. I identified three types of decisions: (1) discretionary decisions, in which teachers had the ability to decide how to get the job done with only loose restrictions on the method and time of their work; (2) collaborative decisions, in which teachers were required to work with colleagues toward a common decision; and (3) leadership decisions, in which teachers were directed to follow explicit instructions.

The respondents—from schools in the United States and Canada—to the initial survey reported that only 4 percent of their classroom decisions were discretionary, 22 percent were collaborative, and 74 percent were top-down leadership directions. While I respect that people's perceptions may seem like their realities, my many observations of organizations suggested that two employees with the same schedule, same budget, same union agreement, and same supervisors were often doing remarkably different things. Therefore, these perceptions seemed far afield of reality. I conducted an experiment in which I observed minute-to-minute decisions by teachers, and the results were striking. For example, many on-the-spot decisions, such as hooking students' interest and identifying the need to provide a quick minilesson or check for understanding, were discretionary. Some decisions, such as using a common formative assessment, were collaborative. Other decisions, such as carrying out district-level assessments and following the district curriculum, were mandatory (Reeves, 2020c). Discretionary decisions comprised 39 percent of the actual decisions, 34 percent of the decisions were collaborative, and 27 percent were the result of top-down leadership direction. How could reality diverge so far from perception? Part of the reason is history. If teachers were used to having broad discretion in nearly every part of their job, then a decrease from 90 percent discretion to 39 percent discretion certainly may have seemed like such a dramatic decline in autonomy that it felt like 4 percent. When leaders had rarely in the past exercised much authority on the actual work of teachers, then an increase from 10 percent to 27 percent leadership decisions may have seemed to be much greater. But there is another cause for these major misperceptions. The leaders in this study had not done an effective job of clarifying precisely which decisions were discretionary, which were collaborative, and which were the province of leadership. They would say things like, "I like to gain consensus on my decisions," and then make a unilateral decision, leaving all those concerned frustrated and angry. They would, in theory, grant discretion to teachers for some decisions, but they never explicitly communicated that discretion. Even the word *collaboration* had different meanings to different leaders, with some believing the perception that collaboration required teachers to confer with colleagues but not necessarily to come to a common decision, while others insisted that collaboration required a high degree of consistency.

In interviewing teachers and administrators in this study, I learned an important leadership lesson: employees can live with top-down leadership decisions, provided they know what they are and the rationale behind them. Said one, "Look, I don't want to vote on fire drills." In other words, on matters of safety, make the call. It's not discretionary whether you wear a hard hat in a construction zone or whether you skip an essential safety drill. Similarly, employees were weary of being hauled into focus groups to discuss the values of the organization when the values, which had long-held and sincere support, had been long established. Therefore, leadership decisions that are neither collaborative nor discretionary should focus on safety and value issues. If equity and fairness are values for you, don't ask for a vote. If safety is at issue, don't ask for a vote. These are the provinces of leadership, and employees who cannot support the safety priorities and values of the organization are not going to be good fits in any business, nonprofit, or school where they are at odds with leadership on these fundamental issues.

The lives of educators and school administrators are, in brief, not ones in which automatons blindly follow commands, and they are not ones in which free agents make their own decisions with no regard for external requirements. Therefore, my suggestion that leaders need not secure buy-in for every decision is not a justification of an authoritarian leadership style but rather a recognition of reality; our professional lives consist of some freedom, some collaboration, and some adherence to externally imposed requirements. They key is that leaders—particularly during a time of change—be very clear about what is discretionary, what is collaborative, and what is a requirement. In my interviews with teachers as part of this study, it was not so much the existence of requirements that bothered them, but a lack of clarity about what was discretionary and what was required. Even when leaders do not have buy-in to their proposed changes, they must at the very least be clear and consistent about their decision-making framework and let teachers know where they have discretion and where they do not.

RETHINK POSITIVE THINKING

Since the early 20th century, motivational speakers have extolled the value of a positive mental attitude, singing the refrain of "dream it and believe it, and then, miraculously, the dreams will come true." This mantra has an intuitive appeal, as it rests on the widely held view that beliefs and attitudes must be changed before behavior can change. Moreover, it's just a lot more pleasant to be around people who possess positive attitudes. There's just one thing wrong with this viewpoint: it is delusionary and counterproductive. As noted earlier in this chapter, the 21st century evidence on change is that behavior precedes belief, not the other way around. Unmasking the fraud of the miracle claims of a positive mental attitude is not, however, a call for dreary pessimism.

There is an alternative to naive optimism and relentless pessimism: *mental contrasting*. Psychology professor Gabriele Oettingen (2014) amassed more than twenty years of research demonstrating that dreams without a dose of realism are futile, and realism without dreams for future change are emotionally devastating. She posits that the right course is to become dreamers and doers through the process of mental contrasting. Effective change depends on identifying specific barriers to the achievement of dreams and goals and then addressing them forthrightly.

Fantasies and daydreams are pleasant. Indeed, they are a welcome relief from reality. Who needs to deal with fear, disappointment, and rejection when all you need is the mysteries of *The Secret* or a spoonful of *Chicken Soup for the Soul*? The reason we must face fear, disappointment, and rejection is that these factors are essential to progress and successful change. The next time you are in an art museum, ask yourself how many first drafts hang on the museum walls. When you read a spectacular book or a moving poem, consider the intense work, including rejection, disappointment, and perseverance, that led to its creation. The same is true of breakthrough discoveries in science and technology. James Dyson (2011) has stated the eponymous Dyson vacuum cleaner was the result of five thousand failures. Thomas Edison, too, one of the most prolific inventors and who transformed life at work and at home with the incandescent light bulb, was known for his persistence through thousands of failures.

When we think of resilience in psychological terms, we think of it as bouncing back from failures and disappointment. A more nuanced understanding of the term comes from metallurgy—the modulus of elasticity. This is the point at which steel beams, such as those holding up a one-hundred-story skyscraper, will bend, as they must during earthquakes, but can then return to their original position. The beam that cannot bend will splinter in an earthquake, and the entire structure will crumble to the ground. The beam that bends too far will fail to support the structure as well. Thus engineers must design the foundations of spectacularly tall buildings with the modulus of elasticity in mind—a foundation that will be neither brittle and unbending nor one that bends so far it cannot return to its original position. Similarly, the starry-eyed optimist can be crushed when life's earthquakes require that he or she bends. The relentless pessimist with the Eeyore-like conviction that his or her place in the world is doomed to failure will bend with every breeze, fall down in life's earthquakes, and never be restored to a position of strength.

Oettingen's (2014) research contradicts prevailing attitudes that fantasies for personal change are often associated with failure, not success. While there is nothing wrong with positive attitudes, the error is in believing that positivity alone will suffice for change and that, like Dorothy clicking her ruby slippers at the end of *The Wizard of Oz*, our magical thinking will make wishes come true. In brief, wishes and dreams aren't by themselves bad but are insufficient to lead to meaningful change. This process of mental contrasting was far more related to improved performance than the idle pursuit of wishes and dreams. The results were similar whether applied to executives in organizations, students (from elementary school through college), or parents. We are almost always engaged in the process of changing ourselves or attempting to change others. Neither elaborate strategic plans nor facile fancies are successful. But mental contrasting allows people and organizations to allocate resources and time in a realistic manner that addresses obstacles while retaining a focus on goals. Oettingen's (2014) research demonstrates that people with the same dreams are dramatically more likely to take specific actions to achieve those dreams if they have a plan that establishes clear conditions, dates, and steps. Transformative-leadership expert Cathy Presland (2018) notes that exclusive reliance on positive feelings results in an abdication of responsibility, precisely the opposite of what we wish to teach students and encourage in our professional colleagues.

CONCLUSION

In this chapter, we initially confronted the myth of buy-in. Though the necessity of buy-in remains an article of faith among management consultants, the faith in this discredited belief is one of the greatest impediments to organizational change. Leaders must consider one of two truths. Either they really do have buy-in, in which case they are not asking for significant change. Or they do not have buy-in, in which case they must decide whether to wait—forever—for the perfect bliss of buy-in, or to proceed with the conviction that the real acceptance of change happens not before the change but after people observe the positive impact of change and only at that point give their acceptance and support to the change. If attitudes and beliefs were all that was necessary for change, then no one would smoke, drink, or eat unhealthy foods because, after all, the evidence against these bad habits is clear. Information is not enough. Successful change depends on the principle that behavior precedes belief. When people exercise, eat and drink judiciously, and stop smoking, within a few weeks they not only feel better but receive external feedback that they look better, act better, and smell better. It is the post-change feelings and feedback that sustain change.

We learned that leaders must be crystal clear about levels of decision making within their organizations. Some decisions are discretionary, some are collaborative, and some of necessity are top-down. The key for effective change leadership is absolute clarity about which decisions fall into each of these three categories. When it comes to top-down leadership decisions that allow for no discretion by employees, the criteria should be safety and values. Once leaders allow discretion in matters of safety, they put lives at risk. Once leaders allow discretion in matters of values, they announce that their values have no meaning. Whatever leaders tolerate—especially with respect to violations of values—they endorse.

Finally, we engaged in a critique of the prevailing model of change that depends excessively on positive thinking without realism. The secret of the universe is not that mystical forces will respond to our wishes but rather that our wishes are vacuous if not accompanied by a serious consideration of experience, obstacles, and thoughtful planning.

REFLECTION

Review the following prompts, and record your responses someplace where you can easily refer to them throughout the deep change journey.

1. Describe a time when you have been surprised—perhaps a person you initially disliked turned out to be a good friend, or an idea that you thought was absurd turned out to be valid. What happened to change your mind?
2. What was the last really difficult task, either personal or professional, that you encountered in which you went from novice to master? In the early stages of learning and mastering this task, how did you overcome your frustrations? What led you to break through to mastery?
3. Consider a change that you know is necessary right now in your school or educational system. Role-play a dialogue with someone who does not believe in this change and is unwilling to implement it. Treating this other person with respect and courtesy, try to focus the dialogue on actions rather than beliefs.

Chapter 4

Getting Ready for Deep Change

Schools and districts are complex, and therefore leaders are wise to consider the degree to which the groups they lead are ready for deep change. Before we explore the more granular details of the deep change model in part 2 (page 53), in this chapter, we'll preview its deliberately sequenced phases—imagining, focusing, implementing, and accelerating. In doing so, we'll learn how to prepare all stakeholders to engage in deep change and how to identify the keys to enactment for a school or district.

IMAGINING

Imagination takes two forms: (1) the positive vision that the change will create and (2) the negative consequences of failing to create that change. The creative process involves engagement in compelling images of the future. The evidence of successful creativity suggests that traditional notions of effective imagination are deeply flawed. For example, a common imaginative process is brainstorming, in which participants offer up ideas without a filter. The cardinal rule of traditional brainstorming sessions is to avoid criticism. Every idea has value. It's an appealing illusion, one that advertising executive Alex F. Osborn (1953) popularized in the 1950s and that remains actively used today. But according to University of

Pennsylvania psychologist and researcher Adam Grant (2016), this sort of brainstorming, however congenial it might be, does not lead to high-quality imaginative discussions. In fact, debate, contention, and critique are essential parts of the creative process. The other misconception about the imaginative process is that it is the leader's responsibility to create the vision. Indeed, the phrase *visionary leader* is one often regarded as a compliment, as if the person in charge is uniquely endowed with imaginative abilities and the job of others is to follow. But the evidence is clear that effective processes for creative imagination are collaborative, not solitary. While the romantic ideal of the lone artist seeking inspiration from the muse is pervasive, it's largely inaccurate. MIT scientist Alex Pentland (2014) finds that collaborative work results in creative breakthroughs far more commonly than the work completed under the mythology of the lone genius. Indeed, Pentland (2014) points out that even great breakthroughs assumed to be the result of solitary work gained that reputation not because of the solitude of the artist, author, or scientist but because he—and I choose my pronouns deliberately—did not share credit with his collaborators. Preparing for deep change, therefore, is the work not of the lone visionary but of a team whose members can collaborate and challenge one another to create both a positive vision of the future and a vision of what the world of their stakeholders will be like if they fail to change.

FOCUSING

A cardinal principle of deep change is that fragmentation is the enemy of success. Therefore, before beginning the deep change process, leaders must create a not-to-do list. That is, they must identify the specific initiatives, activities, meetings, and processes that will be removed from the individuals and teams that they lead. This requires leaders to be clear about what their current number of initiatives is. My experience is that the list is invariably longer than the leader thinks it is. Once leaders have conducted the initiative inventory, it is imperative that they determine which initiatives and practices will be terminated. When I challenge leaders to do this, the most common response I hear is, "I can't take anything off the table. Everything I do is important. And if I do take something off the table, I'll be in trouble." But unless leaders have a magical means of adding more hours to the day, the truth is that they will always have a not-to-do list—but it will be one that is unconscious, with the items simply being those that the leaders and their teams never get to. Far better to have a *consciously* selected not-to-do list that will let faculty, staff, and all stakeholders know that you are serious about focus.

IMPLEMENTING

The implementation phase in deep change is based on the work of the late Harvard Business School professor Clayton M. Christensen, who created a simple but effective model of executive disciplines. Christensen's (as cited in Newport, 2016b) model includes the following four disciplines.

1. **Focus on the wildly important:** It's one thing to talk about priorities, but the wildly important is qualitatively different from the raft of challenges that are merely important. Among the many tasks, meetings, and messages clamoring for the leader's attention, a very few qualify as wildly important.
2. **Act on the lead measures:** In education, it takes time to understand the relationship between the effect of our work—student achievement, attendance, behavior, and so forth—and the causes. Therefore, it is essential to pay attention to the lead measures. Richard DuFour, Rebecca DuFour, and I (2018) suggest that a constructive approach to educational accountability is about looking at not merely the lagging indicators, such as test scores, but the lead measures. In this context, lead measures are the observable actions of teachers and leaders that will lead to improved student results. For example, I may not know about student results until the end of a semester or, in the case of state test scores, until well after the end of the year. But leading indicators can be observed every day. How often did teachers engage in collaborative scoring? How often did leaders make time in faculty meetings for the creation of common formative assessments? How often did teachers outside of English language arts engage in nonfiction writing? These are just a few examples of leading indicators that leaders can track and thereby motivate colleagues and encourage progress. This relates directly to the next discipline.
3. **Keep a compelling scoreboard:** I always smile when well-meaning parents insist from the sidelines of Little League baseball and soccer games that they don't keep score. I would like to burst their bubble and share with them that not only do the kids keep score, but they like keeping score. They can deal with score keeping as long as they know that the game is fair and that they can come and play another day. The same is true of adults. The resistance to score keeping in education is

attributable to the pervasive feeling that the results on the scoreboard are beyond our control. That feeling is completely understandable, as many factors—including poor nutrition; poverty; parental neglect; and access to alcohol, drugs, and guns—are beyond the control of teachers and administrators. So in order for a scoreboard to be compelling, it is essential that the data that go on the scoreboard are factors that we *can* control and improve every day. That's why leading indicators should be most prominent on the scoreboard.

4. **Create a cadence of accountability:** Newport (2016b) suggests that for any team that owns a wildly important goal, there should be clear accountability measures that can be reviewed regularly. Such goals might include attendance, students reading at grade level, and so on. Effective accountability also includes the leading indicators, and effective accountability systems always combine result data with cause data—the leading indicators—so that leaders and staff can see the relationship between the two. But there is the critical matter of communicating what *accountability* means, as the term is often perceived as threatening. The best way to express accountability in a constructive manner is as follows:

   > *We are not accountable for data–that's like air temperature, just something that is. But we are responsible for how we respond to data. If the temperature is twenty below zero and we don't take precautions to safeguard students, then we're responsible for that response. Similarly, if we have students who are severely behind in core skills or who are chronically absent, then we are accountable for how we respond to that information.*

ACCELERATING

The final phase of the deep change model is acceleration. The hallmark of some five-year strategic plans is lethargy. The flurry of activity required to create the plan is followed by a regression to a slower pace and, over time, the accumulation of more initiatives and tasks that create what organizational design experts Michael Mankins and Eric Garton (2017) call *organizational drag*. The primary resources that we have, they argue, are time, talent, and energy, and when organizations lose focus, they squander these precious resources. By contrast, the commitment to acceleration is exemplified in what Robert Eaker and I (2019) call *100-day leaders*. Whether it is dramatically reducing failures in a single semester, writing the U.S. Constitution, or crafting a great novel, history teaches us that great things can be accomplished in one hundred days. This time frame not only creates a continued sense of focus for educational stakeholders but also allows for midcourse corrections. What if our leading indicators are not as related to our results as we had hoped? We need not wait years to fix that; we can make corrections every one hundred days—or even sooner. Acceleration keeps leaders and everyone in the school focused on what matters most, and it militates against the addition of extraneous diversions of time and resources.

CONCLUSION

Once you have created a collaborative team to imagine both positive and negative futures, demonstrated a commitment to focus by establishing the not-to-do list for every part of the school and district, established your implementation disciplines, and scheduled 100-day cycles of review and further focus, then you are ready to proceed with deep change. Exactly how to do that is the subject of part 2.

REFLECTION

Review the following prompts, and record your responses someplace where you can easily refer to them throughout the deep change journey.

1. Who will be on your imagination team? Will they bring contrasting views and feel safe in challenging one another, including the leader? Is the leader willing to have his or her vision challenged? If the present vision is a non-negotiable item and not subject to discussion, then leaders should not expect any more than glum compliance from colleagues. While buy-in or consensus is not necessary for deep change success, respect and inclusion are essential.
2. What will be on your not-to-do list? Think not only of major initiatives to terminate but of minor practices to modify. Seemingly small things, like meetings, premeeting protocols, email and text protocols, and expected response times, can have a dramatic impact on creating the time and resources that deep change will require.
3. As you consider the four disciplines of execution, what are the barriers to successful implementation? For example, does the school or district have a history with negative and intimidating accountability systems? Were scorecards used in a punitive way?

How can you learn from those mistakes to make the disciplines of execution for deep change more effective?

4. What are examples of successful short-term goals in your school and district? What are important things that you and your colleagues achieved in one hundred or fewer days? How did you celebrate those accomplishments? In terms of morale and collaborative learning, how is the 100-day cycle different from accountability cycles of a year or longer?

PART 2

THE DEEP CHANGE MODEL

The deep change leadership model is based on four phases—(1) imagining, (2) focusing, (3) implementing, and (4) accelerating—and each phase stands in stark contrast to traditional change models. In the imagining phase, the vision of the charismatic leader is replaced with two divergent images of the future: one that reflects the compelling benefits of the change and one that vividly captures a future in which the change has not been implemented. In the focusing phase, leaders not only compare options of alternative change plans but also explicitly decide what they and the schools they lead will stop doing. While traditional change models often attempt to blend the ideas of many stakeholders, typically represented in a guiding coalition, the deep change model requires choices among mutually exclusive options. While traditional change models are additive, with one assessment, curriculum, or technology initiative piled on top of existing initiatives, the deep change model requires that no new initiatives be added without the removal of existing ones. In the implementing phase, leaders follow the four disciplines of execution to monitor both the results of their actions and the leading indicators—that is, the observable actions of staff to create those results. While advocates of traditional change models often take pride in focusing on results, the deep change model is based on the premise that the measurement of results is meaningless without an understanding of the causes of those results. In the accelerating phase, the momentum of change continues through a series of 100-day cycles. This is in sharp contrast to the time horizon of traditional change models, which often last years.

Before beginning the process of deep change, leaders have the obligation to reassure stakeholders about what will not change, a subject we explore in chapter 5. This counters the perception that once a new change initiative begins, *everything* changes, which creates unnecessary anxiety and stress among staff and stakeholders. Change is challenging enough without adding to the pain and confusion by giving the impression that there is nothing left but the ashes of the past. Even in schools facing great difficulties, leaders can almost always find values, traditions, and practices that are worthy of respect and support. In chapters 6 through 9, we dive into the four phases of the deep change model.

Chapter 5

Deciding What Does Not Change

Change leaders are often so focused on what they wish to change that they forget the first rule of change: decide what will not change. Almost every school or district, even those in crisis, have characteristics that are worthy of preservation. These might include positive relationships with teachers or students. Perhaps there are long-held traditions and values that are part of the cultural identity of the school or district that are worth keeping. Before leaders announce changes in the organizational chart, location of desks, and assignment of roles, it is essential that they clarify what will not change. This chapter explores the factors that leaders should not and, in some cases, cannot change; humankind's drive for competence; change with design thinking in mind; the necessity for leaders to focus on managing and changing themselves as an integral part of changing their schools and districts; and lessons from personal change.

WHAT WE CANNOT CHANGE

Psychotherapist David Richo (2014) convincingly demonstrates that the realities of life supersede our desire to change. This is not a message of the futility of change leadership but rather a clarion call to focus our change efforts on the areas where change is possible. In the words of the Serenity Prayer, often attributed to 20th century theologian Reinhold Niebuhr but possibly composed earlier by other authors (as cited in Goodstein, 2008), "God, grant me the serenity to accept the things I cannot change, the courage to change the things I can, and the wisdom to know the difference." This prayer expresses sentiments that have resonance with anyone secular or religious who is engaged in individual or organizational change.

Richo (2014) articulates five facts of life that we cannot change and must accept. Let's consider each of them in the context of education.

1. **Everything changes and ends:** While certain elements of education are strongly rooted in tradition, any educator with more than a few years of experience will be able to observe changes in the profession. During the pandemic of 2020, technological solutions abruptly ended the tradition of instruction taking place only in the classroom. But Clayton M. Christensen and colleagues (2011) had predicted this in their aptly titled book *Disrupting Class,* in which the authors argue that technological solutions will fundamentally change the delivery of classroom instruction. During the two decades preceding the pandemic of 2020, I observed teachers experimenting with flipped classrooms, in which students watched lectures and other content on video, and class time was devoted to student-teacher interactions, which included students' questions and teachers' checks for understanding. The phenomenon that everything changes and ends applies to technology. Ask teenagers, as I have done, why they don't respond to emails, and they'll look at you as if you've asked why they don't respond to drawings on the side of a cave. Group chats, texts, and Instagram have largely replaced email for the teens with whom I spoke with in 2020, and in time, those methods will join their ancient predecessors.
2. **Things do not always go according to plan:** Schools routinely invest in a new curriculum program, and with substantial resources devoted to supplies and workshops, leaders assume that the program has been implemented. But the reality is that implementation takes place on a spectrum from the delivery of supplies and training, to tentative application of the program with students, to delivery of the program with evidence that the program has influenced student learning, to schoolwide and system-wide deep implementation and continuous learning. But there are many bumps along the road from delivery to full implementation, including staff changes, competing

initiatives, and, most commonly, the failure to remove previous curriculum and activities that prevent the new program from being implemented.

3. **Life is not always fair:** Educators and school administrators have little difficulty explaining this truism to students, but they often have trouble applying the maxim to themselves and to colleagues. Perhaps the greatest source of unfairness in education is the ridicule to which teachers and the entire education system are subjected for reasons that have more to do with the eighteen hours per day that students spend outside school than with the six hours each day that they spend in school. It's quite true that poor student results may be due to ineffective teaching and leadership, but to ignore that some of the causes of low performance are related to food insecurity, sleep deprivation, and substance abuse is to deny the reality that I have seen schools face around the world. This is another reason that leading indicators are so important. We must be accountable for our professional practices. It is not fair to hold ourselves accountable for the actions and inactions of parents during, for example, the early-morning hours before students come to school.
4. **Pain is part of life:** Psychologist Angela Duckworth (2016) studied first-year students at West Point who, under those difficult and painful circumstances, survived the experience and thrived in school. She found that grit—a combination of variables including persistence through pain and discomfort—was a better predictor of success than either intellectual or physical ability. These findings are in stark contrast to the concerns I have heard from teachers who speak of *snowplow parents*—those who smooth the road for their children. However well-intentioned such parents may be, they are only delaying the pain that will be part of their children's lives, not helping their children steer clear of it altogether. Schools rightly avoid deliberate infliction of pain, such as bullying and intimidation at the hands of students and adults. But educators make a grave error when they protect students from the honest feedback that they must improve their present level of work. For the student who has never been asked to rewrite a paper, resubmit a lab report, or work harder in any endeavor, the idea that his or her work is less than perfect may come as a shock. My own findings (Reeves, 2019) suggest that educators' inclination to prevent students from

experiencing this type of pain has a particularly adverse effect on girls and young women. The expectation of perfection from our daughters begins when they are young, and the conviction that anything less than perfect performance is shameful prevents them from taking on challenges that might result in negative feedback. This inhibits their performance years into the future.

5. **People are not loving and loyal all the time:** Students and many adults sometimes confuse disagreement with a lack of love and loyalty. That is because they mistakenly view criticism of work as an attack on the person. Because the impulse to social cohesion and the aversion to conflict are so strong, I have heard middle school students say, "I knew that my friend made a mistake in her essay, but I didn't want to tell her because it would hurt her feelings." That sort of honest criticism is qualitatively different from cyberbullying in which a student is called stupid. We must therefore encourage our students and our colleagues to stand up for principles but not to get into the swamp of internet combat in reaction to every insult. It is important that we model civil disagreement in educational contexts. In classrooms and professional conferences, debate is a wonderful way to exchange divergent ideas without personal attacks. While many teachers offer structured debates in their classrooms, I have seen only a handful of public disagreements in professional conferences. By embracing debate, we could demonstrate that disagreement is not the same as disrespect or disloyalty.

While these may seem obvious on reflection, amid the challenges of change leadership, the persistence of these five unchangeable factors often astonish us. We seek earnestly to avoid endings, are surprised by the derailment of an elegantly established plan, and harbor deep resentment toward the unfairness of people and of life in general. We hear the Buddha say that life is suffering, but surely that is for other people, because we avoid pain at all costs. And we are shocked and disappointed when the people we know best—our family members, colleagues, and trusted friends—don't appear to be loving and loyal all the time. We tend to magnify disappointment over satisfaction and failure over success.

THE DRIVE FOR COMPETENCE

One element of the human psyche that is unlikely to change is the drive for competence. It is an essential element of human motivation. This offers change leaders the opportunity to simultaneously value the drive for competence while also requiring colleagues to improve their levels of performance. People will strive for competence, but only as long as the performance standard is clear and the effort toward reaching that standard is clearly related to success. Babies will fall a thousand times as they learn to walk, but they see and feel incremental progress with each attempt. The same is true of musicians, athletes, surgeons, students, factory workers, truck drivers, and people who aspire to high levels of performance in any field. Psychologist Anders Ericsson and science writer Robert Pool (2016) conclude that what all these efforts have in common is not just practice but deliberate practice. If all that were needed for expertise was the oft-quoted ten thousand hours (Gladwell, 2008), one might think weekend golfers would have a lower handicap at age fifty-five than at age twenty-five, but that is rarely the case. They swing at the ball in the same way decade after decade, expressing frustrations with their misses but not investing the time and effort into receiving explicit feedback and, incrementally, applying that feedback to improve each tiny element of their stroke. This is why the world's greatest performers in any endeavor—music, sports, acting, and writing—have coaches and work with unrelenting focus on improving their performance. They maintain their motivation because they know and can objectively observe that they are getting better all the time. They quit either when they know that they are no longer improving or when they have become at peace with a lack of improvement.

The notion that we can get better with experience—what professor Teresa Amabile and developmental psychologist Steven Kramer (2011) call the *progress principle*—is what motivates people, from infants to high-performing professionals. Whether it is the progress from crawling to walking, getting to the next level of a video game, or the refinement of a speech to thousands of employees, the motivating principle behind effective practice is the belief that we are making progress. People who seek to make progress and the deliberate practice that it entails often seek to make the activity fun. But that completely misses the point. As John Hattie (2009) demonstrates based on a synthesis of tens of thousands of studies, deliberate practice is not fun. People who succeed continue to engage in deliberate practice not for the joy of the practice itself but rather as a result of the sense of progress that deliberate practice yields.

CHANGE BY DESIGN

Tim Brown is the CEO of IDEO, one of the most innovative companies in the world. In his book *Change by Design*, he documents the impact of applying *design thinking* to some of the most complex organizational challenges in the world, from technology to health care to government to education (Brown, 2019). Design thinking takes the perspective of the end user. For example, design thinking in curriculum is less about what the publisher wants to deliver and more about the student who must experience the curriculum. Design thinking in technology is less about the sophistication of the product and more about how the teacher or student using the technology will apply it. At its essence, design thinking incorporates not only functionality—like the first Apple mouse—but the beauty and delight that users experience with a product or practice that is useful, as well as evocative of joy and satisfaction. Because change is so difficult, the approach of change by design seeks to give change leaders a tool that uses attraction rather than compulsion. Massive transformations that have been accomplished on a broad scale—from snail mail to email, from early personal websites to pervasive social media, from access to information measured in days or weeks to responses to inquiries measured in microseconds—have been accomplished not by doing battle through barriers that require dogged persistence to overcome but rather by making the alternatives so attractive that one feels foolish for not using them.

My mother was born in 1922, two years after women received the right to vote through the ratification of the Nineteenth Amendment to the U.S. Constitution. She was born into a world in which Charles Lindbergh had not yet flown across the Atlantic, car ownership was exceptional, and parents worried that radio shows would disrupt the concentration of children who were better off focusing on schoolwork. She is also on social media and email every day in her late nineties. Brown (2019) explains the pace of change with the claim that the farmer in 1750 CE had more in common with a farmer in 1750 BCE than he did with his own grandchildren. For my mother to engage in modern technology, such as email or interactive video, she would read manuals, take classes, and spend hours with customer support. My mother's grandchildren, by contrast, have not known a world without the internet. For them, as beneficiaries of design thinking, if a device is not intuitive—that is, if they cannot use it without instructions—then it is discarded as a waste of time.

With regard to the impact of technology in the 21st century, it is important to note that the massive quantity of change is not the result of greater numbers of successful changes. Rather, it is that change is so frequent, failure is so frequent, and recovery from failure is so pervasive that it is more accurate to say that while the change process has improved, the fundamental resistance to change and the spectacular failures associated with change remain as pervasive now as ever. In brief, change is happening more quickly not because we are so brilliant but because we are more bullheaded and persistent. The problems that change leaders are attacking have grown in complexity over the years, and with complexity comes an exponential increase in the number of ways a proposed change can fail.

The challenges of design thinking in deep change are not merely an artifact of technology. Printed text has existed for at least five millennia, yet very smart and creative people continue to produce typefaces that are easier to read. Kings have sat on the best thrones money could buy for longer than that, yet we still strive to design a comfortable chair. Schools have been around since before the Lyceum, yet school improvement remains the focus of many societies. Some would argue that since the Athenians first practiced democracy, modern societies still flounder in achieving a governance structure that meets the needs of at least the majority of citizens, an aspiration as old as the ancient philosophers who attempted to design it. Thus, change by design is not merely about a particular product or process but rather about the way in which we pursue and implement change, from the first glimpse of an idea through the many iterations of development that follow. The key to the insights associated with design thinking is user-centered research. Although market research is hardly a new concept, a surprising amount of traditional research rests on a surprisingly unhelpful technique—asking prospective users what they want. While this may seem intuitively obvious, design thinking reveals a stark difference between what users say they want and what they actually do. IDEO researchers, for example, don't begin with a definition of the problem but rather embed themselves deeply in the user experience, whether that experience is as a consumer, driver, commuter, factory worker, student, or executive. For example, would desks in schools look and feel different if the executives of furniture manufacturers and the designers they employ were required to sit in current desks for six hours a day, five consecutive days? Would school schedules be different if senior administrators were required to sit in an algebra class and, just as they were about to ask questions about the mathematics they could not recall from their high school days, a bell rang? How different would the history curriculum be if textbook publishers were required to read and answer questions on the massive books that they publish? These insights reveal a nuanced definition of the problem that designers must consider and leads to a deeper understanding of the nature and magnitude of the changes that must be made (Ellen MacArthur Foundation & IDEO, n.d.). The importance of defining the problem is summed up in an idea often misattributed to Albert Einstein: "If I had only an hour to solve a problem, I would spend fifty-five minutes defining the problem and then five minutes solving it" (Quote Investigator, 2014). Even if Einstein did not say this, the advice is sound. The essence of change by design is understanding what we seek to change.

SELF-MANAGEMENT AND CREDIBILITY

Leadership hypocrisy is neither a new nor insightful concept. Nothing breeds more cynicism and distrust among employees and stakeholders than a leader's unstated message that "I'm perfect; it's everyone else who needs to change." James M. Kouzes and Barry Z. Posner (2012) have had a profound influence on leadership since the 1980s. Their research on credibility (Kouzes & Posner, 2011) provides clear and convincing evidence that teachers, students, and parents will forgive leaders for errors in data analysis, strategic planning, communication, and a host of other failings if the leaders have credibility. Leaders who admit their mistakes quickly and honestly and, most importantly, do what they say they will do earn credibility every day. By contrast, leaders who demand open communication from others but operate the C-suite behind a veil of secrecy, who demand frugality from others but squander organizational resources on lavish perks for themselves, and who demand accountability from others but fail to follow through on their promises have squandered the leader's most precious resource: credibility. Thus, the unending job of the leader is the relentless challenge of self-management, closing the gap between our core beliefs and values and our actions. While the prescription of "do what you say you will do" seems simple, the daily adherence to this injunction, when taken seriously, is a challenge.

Credibility and the self-management that it requires entail a daily discipline of promises made and promises kept. Every meeting led by a credible leader ends with clear and public commitments, and the next meeting begins with a consistent theme: "In our last meeting, I made these commitments, and here is how I have kept those commitments." In the event a commitment is not kept, this too is a matter of open declaration and not concealment. When a promise is not kept, there is no excuse making or temporizing but rather a candid admission that the leader failed, acknowledges the failure, and will address the failure immediately and publicly. The purpose of this exercise is neither humiliation nor needless self-flagellation but the endless pursuit of the candor and integrity on which effective leadership depends.

Effective leaders share their organizational and personal goals so that they model the accountability they seek from others. They publicly share their commitments to respecting the time of others by reducing the quantity and increasing the quality of meetings. As author Nir Eyal (2019) explains, they share their goals of greater focus by disclosing their techniques for distraction-free times of the day and week. They share their commitment to health, wellness, and family, not as a means of shaming others but rather as a way to acknowledge their own imperfections and need for improvement. When, as happens with more than 80 percent of New Year's resolutions, they get off track, according to journalist Lindsay Dodgson (2018), they admit it and share candidly the road back to the pursuit of their goals. In order to create and sustain a learning environment, leaders and educators must maintain a regular practice of not only acknowledging their mistakes but sharing publicly what they learned from those mistakes. For example, they might say:

> *When I first saw the large number of failures by students, I assumed that it was because of poor attendance and, in essence, blamed the students and their families for failing to come to school. But a deeper dive into the data showed me that a substantial number of those failures were occurring with students who have 90 percent or better attendance rates. It made me stop blaming the students and start thinking about how we can provide better feedback and support to struggling students.*

While they need not flaunt their successes, they share them in a matter-of-fact way so that every colleague knows of their commitment to self-management. Change leaders depend not on grand plans or rhetorical flourishes but on the credibility that stems from personal commitment and modeling.

LESSONS FROM PERSONAL CHANGE

Although the statistics on organizational and personal change are discouraging, there are wonderful examples of success that should give us hope. It is important to note that our inspiration does not lie solely in the successes of others. Even though the vast majority of us can be tempted to dwell on the New Year's resolutions not kept and promises to ourselves we have broken, we have also had successes. Take a moment to reflect on the goals that you set and achieved: to get a job, establish a relationship, or serve others. Think of the bad habits that you have successfully ended. Think of the many promises to yourself and others that you have kept. Tom Rath (2007) convincingly demonstrates that for both personal and organizational progress, the most effective strategy is to identify our strengths and maximize those. Unfortunately, most people play a lifelong game of whack-a-mole in which they are perseverating about one weakness after another. This is a prescription for futility and hopelessness. The point is not that we should ignore our weaknesses. If you are smoking, quit. If you are overweight, watch what you eat and get some exercise. But if these typically simplistic solutions have not worked—and they do not work for the vast majority of people—then consider a different approach. As James Clear (2018) demonstrates in *Atomic Habits*, it is essential that we not just quit a bad habit but rather replace it with something we genuinely enjoy. I do not enjoy exercise, but I love watching comedy shows. When I adjusted my routine to only watch reruns of comedies when I was exercising, it quickly eliminated the negative associations I had with exercise and replaced it with the joyful opportunity to watch my favorite comedies. I do not enjoy kale or any number of other foods that experts say are healthy. The only way I could learn to enjoy kale would be to put it in a deep fryer and then drown it in hot fudge, which probably defeats the purpose of eating kale in the first place. But what I can do is to explore the wide variety of foods that are equally healthy but that have flavor and texture that are somewhat superior to munching on paper towels. It took some time and experimentation, but I found a wonderful variety of foods, including some of my favorite Indian and Thai dishes, that met my needs for healthy alternatives to deep-fried and fudge-covered kale.

You can identify and build on your strengths, using them to replace the futility and dreary anxiety associated with focusing on weaknesses. There are many commercial assessments to help you find your strengths, including the most widely used Gallup's *Strengths Finder 2.0* (Rath, 2007). A very extensive assessment is available for free at the University of Pennsylvania's Authentic Happiness website (www.authentichappiness.org). The content on the site is based on decades of research from the founder of positive psychology, Martin E. P. Seligman (2018).

Just as it is essential for individuals to understand and build on their strengths, the same is true of schools and districts. Those that are most successful know what they are and where they can aspire to be the best. They do not try to be all things to all educators and students. When they stray from the focused path of being the best at what they do and instead attempt to satisfy every stakeholder in every context, schools and districts sacrifice the commitment to excellence that requires intense focus and is the key to sustained success. Buckingham Browne & Nichols School (BB&N), one of the world's elite academic K–12 schools and where my daughter is a student, does not allow students to take eight or nine classes per day—increasingly the norm in many low-performing schools—because BB&N is committed to giving teachers and students the time necessary to achieve excellence in a few things. Everybody Matters, a fast-growing nonprofit based in Phoenix, Arizona, has a brilliant and energetic leader, Lori Madrid, who surely could accomplish social good in a wide variety of areas. But her success is partly the result of a relentless focus on the core mission of serving the emotional needs of students in inner-city schools and training the next generation of social workers and therapists to meet these needs. By contrast, the business, education, and nonprofit worlds are littered with examples of organizations that, in pursuit of diversification, provide mediocrity on a grand scale. Swarthmore psychologist

Barry Schwartz (2016) examines the dangers of pursuing too much variety in *The Paradox of Choice*. People enjoy choice—but only to a certain extent. He offers the simple example of people buying jam from a display with four, six, or eight alternatives. Consumers evaluated the alternatives, made their choice, and moved on. But as the number of choices expanded, the probability that consumers would enjoy the variety and make a purchase declined. Indeed, when choices were expanded to thirty-two choices, consumers were overwhelmed and purchased nothing. The endless task lists, timelines, and overloaded communication environments in which most educators, schools, and districts operate are antithetical to the focus that is essential for success.

Consider some examples of successful change, and notice the commonalities among them, despite widely varying contexts, personalities, and missions. Robert Pondiscio (2019) documents the exceptional and sustained results students achieve in New York's Success Academy Schools. This network of schools is larger than most public school districts in the United States, and the students are largely from low-income families and are members of ethnic and linguistic minorities. If achievement were to fit the national profile for these student demographics, reading and mathematics scores would be abysmal, the dropout rate high, and teacher turnover rampant. Yet for more than a decade, their results compare favorably with wealthy New York suburbs, such as Scarsdale. There is no magic formula but rather a relentless focus on consistency in curriculum, instruction, behavioral expectations, and parent involvement.

CONCLUSION

At the core of change leadership is the candid admission of what we cannot change. These immutable factors include not only the deeply rooted elements of our psyche, such as the drive for competence, but also the facts of the universe that fly in the face of our fantasies. We cannot change, for example, the unfairness and pain that life brings to all of us. In order to lead change effectively, we must learn from the tenets of design thinking, pursuing utility, beauty, and accessibility. Most importantly, before designing any change, we must engage in extreme empathy, understanding the problem from the perspective of others, especially those who will be most affected by the change we are advocating. Finally, change leaders must first lead themselves, engaging in the daily challenge of establishing and re-establishing credibility. They share their foibles and successes, taking personal responsibility for the former and sharing credit for the latter.

REFLECTION

Review the following prompts, and record your responses someplace where you can easily refer to them throughout the deep change journey.

1. Describe your own context for a personal change effort. Think of a specific change you would like to make—improved student engagement, better access to technology, more creative teaching strategies, or whatever is most important for you. As you consider the context, describe the three categories of factors that will influence your success: (1) factors you can neither control nor influence, (2) factors you can influence but not control, and (3) factors you can both influence and control. It will be helpful to list those in writing.
2. Focusing just on the third category—factors you can both influence and control—describe one or two specific actions you can take in the next twenty-four hours in pursuit of your change goal. For example, if you want to improve student engagement, you cannot control whether students come to school sober and well rested; whether they have access to alcohol, tobacco, drugs, and guns; and whether they are up at three in the morning checking social media. These are factors completely out of your control. But you can control the strategies you use for engaging every student, whether in the classroom or in a virtual environment. You control the physical locations of teachers and students. You can control the degree to which feedback to students and teachers is constructive, accurate, and timely.

Chapter 6

Imagining

The first phase of deep change is to imagine both the positive future associated with change and the negative future associated with failure to change. Traditional change efforts embrace a vision process, but it is usually focused only on the positive. However, in order to facilitate stakeholders' passionate and purposeful engagement, on which deep change depends, it is necessary to recognize that passion stems not only from hope for the positive but from fear of the negative. This chapter is about the distinction between passion—pursuing one's heart's desire of the moment—and the lifelong pursuit of purpose. When properly channeled, passion can drive us to new heights, sustaining us when conditions are difficult, time is short, and relationships are frayed. Passion can serve as an inspiration, the intrinsic motivation that far exceeds the motivation entailed in compensation and accolades. In order to lead an environment of sustained deep change, stakeholders' passion must be persistent, not transitory. Passion is more than passing enthusiasm, like a teenager in the thrall of a new band. Persistent passion helps us to maintain focus even as many other priorities clamor for our attention. This chapter suggests replacing the ephemeral pursuit of passion with the more deep, complex, and challenging task of pursuing passion with a purpose. This pursuit is less catching butterflies in the net while walking through the fields of splendor and more confronting dragons in the dark of night, not always accompanied by magical swords and shields. It is difficult, emotionally dangerous, and often disappointing work. Psychologist Marc Schoen (2013) suggests that the ability to accept high levels of discomfort is the key to not only effective change but also serenity and psychological health. Also, as Stephanie Lee (2019) argues, passions can and should change over time as we learn and grow.

Passion is not always pleasant, and passionate anger, a deeply troubling emotion, can be an important source of effective change when it is appropriately directed at the forces that deserve our most intense opposition. We will confront people in schools and districts who sincerely do not value safety, equity, and truth, and who do not, as it were, play by the Queensberry rules of boxing. These are the people, forces, and movements that must be met not only with effective strategy but with passionate anger, an emotion we possess when we find things *as they are* not merely disadvantageous but dangerous, offensive, and morally unacceptable.

Let's take a more in-depth look at imagination as a catalyst to deep change, passion with a purpose, and the idea of constructive, passionate anger.

IMAGINATION AS A CATALYST TO DEEP CHANGE

Grant (2016) argues that there is a clear relationship between generating imaginative ideas and achieving deep change. In fields as diverse as sports, business, and education, Grant's (2016) research suggests a quantity-quality relationship: "The best way to boost your originality," he concludes, "is to produce more ideas" (p. 245). Rather than offering up brainstorming, though, which can result in a number of unusable ideas, Grant (2016) argues for imagination with a purpose. In order to avoid dull repetition of previous images, he recommends strategies that provide different perspectives, such as immersing ourselves in a new domain of learning, seeking more feedback from peers, and deliberately considering reasons why our ideas will not work. Many vision statements I've seen are not credible because they are not only full of ambiguity; they appear never to have been considered by anything less than an uncritical audience. For the imagining phase of deep change to be credible, it must have stood the test of multiple perspectives and thoughtful critiques.

When we engage in the imaginative process, the enthusiasm and passion of others can be alluring. We envision joyous students, committed teachers, and happy parents and administrators engaged in the pursuit of learning. It's fun to watch top professionals at work and imagine that all our schools would be like that.

We enjoy and are motivated to pursue the areas where we are most competent, where we can work without noticing the passage of time, engaged in what pioneering psychologist Mihaly Csikszentmihalyi (1990) calls *flow.* Before the athlete, teacher, executive, musician, or writer ever attained the state of flow, however, there were many hours of difficult and challenging work. Indeed, one of the most overlooked hallmarks of successful creative endeavors is trial and error (Reeves & Reeves, 2017). As enjoyable as it is to imagine a future of happy and contented colleagues and students, the failure to contemplate the hard work, including the many trials and errors along the way, that precedes deep change will undermine the very change efforts we seek.

Entrepreneur and *Forbes* contributor Susan O'Brien (2019) notes that passions can develop from strengths, and it takes some time and experimentation to find those strengths. Moreover, the things that many people are passionate about—traveling, cooking, and spending time with family—are not necessarily consistent with career goals outside of reality television, the pursuit of which may diminish one's enthusiasm for traveling, cooking, and spending time with family. Similarly, teachers often have rosy imaginations about their role as teachers. Perhaps they recall their favorite teacher, whom they loved as much as a parent and from whom they felt that love reciprocated. But now, in their first jobs as classroom educators, the environment may be strikingly different, with apathetic students, caustic parents, and unsupportive administrators. Administrators, too, sometimes take charge of a school, confident in their ability to make changes based on the rightness of their cause. But they can be overwhelmed by administrative demands and institutional resistance to change. Add to these stressors the fact that many teachers graduate from college with six-figure debt and have a job with a five-figure income. Carolyn Gregoire (2013), writing in the *HuffPost,* echoes this concern. It's hard to find one's bliss, she argues, if one is broke, unemployed, and living in the room he or she occupied as a teenager. This does not, she adds, mean that the pursuit of financial security requires the abandonment of passion. Rather, we must be clearheaded about how the rest of our lives, including work and family, are consistent with our pursuit of passion. If passion is not to be found in the workplace, for example, it's important to have a job that allows time for volunteer work, family engagement, creative endeavors, or other sources of passion. Work itself can be a wonderful source of passion, provided we are open to new learning. The bliss we imagined in our twenties may not be the bliss we find in creating jobs, nurturing the dreams of others, and helping colleagues grow. Moreover, there are enormous opportunities for Csikszentmihalyi's flow simply by being great at what we do.

PASSION WITH A PURPOSE

For the change leaders, passion is a necessary but insufficient condition for personal and organizational transformation. Martin E. P. Seligman, founder of the positive psychology movement, took enormous risks as a graduate student and junior faculty member to challenge the prevailing orthodoxy, behaviorism, that prevailed in the 1950s and 1960s. He argued, with varying degrees of success, that humans and many animals acted not merely in response to stimuli—pleasure and pain—but with deliberate intention. In a career spanning more than a half century, he routinely encountered and ultimately overcame a barrage of criticism and potentially career-ending threats (Seligman, 2018). Lesser known, however, is how Seligman himself made midcourse corrections throughout his career, ultimately proceeding from his foundational work in learned helplessness to a psychology that held out hope of optimism and happiness. He was motivated, he said, by the urgent need to relieve human suffering, particularly that associated with depression and other mental illnesses. His purpose was not to win arguments, tenure, or publications but to understand and ultimately cure afflictions of the mind that debilitated millions of people around the globe.

Educational leaders can also find passion and purpose. We seek not only improved achievement, frequently mismeasured in test scores alone; we seek to have a lifelong impact on students who will carry our messages of integrity, resilience, and purpose for many decades after graduation. We also find passion and purpose in the support provided to classroom educators, from the shell-shocked new teachers trying to stay one page ahead of students to the veteran who might be discouraged and exhausted with the many ways in which the profession has changed. Having experienced an unprecedented modern pandemic, people involved in education—teachers, students, parents, and leaders—are exhausted. Policies will not give them the renewal that they need, but passion and purpose have the potential to provide that.

How, after especially challenging times, can change leaders recover passion and purpose? Consider the teachers who were deeply invested in their relationships with their students in 2019, having begun every day with handshakes or hugs, and by the end of 2020 were starved for a glimmer of those relationships. During the pandemic of 2020, I saw young students holding a telephone in one hand and a picture of their teacher in the other. These types of scenes are rarely featured in a strategic plan, and I have yet to see the emotional ties between student and teacher reflected in a school accountability report. As leaders imagine the future of deep change, they can and must include these missing human elements. They can, for example, consider the use of specific social and emotional learning strategies as one of their leading indicators, thus demonstrating that the purpose of improved performance is directly related to the passion associated with our deep care for our students.

CONSTRUCTIVE ANGER

The meaning of our lives can sometimes be measured in what makes us angry. Petty people get angry about petty things—inattentive drivers and pedestrians, inconsiderate shoppers, slow service in restaurants, and a host of other irritants that most people find annoying but that lead others into deep paroxysms of rage. Serious people reserve their anger for serious things, such as injustice, threats to children, and violations of values, to name a few. Change leaders in particular reserve their anger for things they want to change, while ineffective leaders direct their anger at things that cannot be changed. Psychologist Marcia Reynolds (2011) notes that the things we wish to change, from personal habits to organizational culture, did not come to be by accident. Teaching and leadership practices that we now wish to change were the result not of carelessness but of deliberation. While it may seem obvious to some that hour-long lectures without checks for understanding are ineffective pedagogy in 2021, the purveyors of those lectures deliver them not out of malice or laziness but because that very method of instruction worked well for them as students. The leaders who bring lofty but vacuous inspirational quotes to faculty meetings are not dunces; they are replicating the leaders they have admired. Every behavior is deliberate, established because it provides comfort, convenience, and some sort of pleasure. This is even true of addictive behaviors that, however destructive, began with deliberate choices that relieved some sort of discomfort. Reynolds (2011) argues that in order for change to take place, our level of anger must exceed the level of comfort, convenience, and pleasure provided by the factors we wish to change. In sum, it's not enough to provide a cost-benefit analysis to generate deep change. We need a change in perspective that will make us sufficiently uncomfortable, even angry, to change our ingrained patterns of behavior. The late Grant Wiggins gave me one of the best examples of this (Reeves, 2016).

Wiggins's daughter, Alexis, was a veteran instructional coach in a very high-performing school and shadowed a student for two days. The context was that teachers were elite professionals, at the top of their game, and the high performance of their students validated their success. And in this context, there would seem to be little reason to change. Yet a mere two days of walking in the footsteps of students demonstrated to Alexis, among other things, that students were leading lives of crushing boredom, sullenly complying with teachers' demands, and not nearly as engaged as the faculty and administration thought (Reeves, 2016). If you want to engender constructive anger among faculty and administrators that will lead them to imagine a better future for a school or district, ask them to replicate this exercise; students' perspectives are dramatically different from what an observer—always standing rather than sitting at an uncomfortable desk—might see and feel.

There are, however, extensive social inhibitions to anger, and this is particularly true of women in leadership positions. Men who express anger are assertive and powerful leaders; women who do the same are labeled as strident, shrill, and inappropriate. This gender-based culture starts very early (Reeves, 2019) and is an echo of the message that children hear: "If you can't say anything nice, don't say anything at all." This refrain, particularly aimed at girls and young women, prevents our daughters from learning how to give and receive effective feedback, and it inhibits the necessary expression of anger and dissatisfaction when women occupy leadership positions later in life.

In order to use anger constructively, it is essential to differentiate the conditions and behaviors that rightfully deserve our anger from the people who promote those conditions and exhibit those behaviors. There are, to be sure, evil people who deserve our deepest condemnation, but the vast majority of the things we wish to change in our lives and our organizations are not the result of evil but the result of a combination of satisfaction, comfort, indifference, and ignorance. Some schools maintain and tolerate toxic cultures because, at least in the short term, those cultures meet people's needs. The boss may be a jerk, people reason, but at least you know where you stand. The culture is toxic, but you are able to take your family on a vacation and pay the mortgage. As Reynolds (2011) suggests, in many people's minds, the benefits of tolerating toxicity exceed the costs of getting angry about it. This leads to deeply held, long-lasting, and toxic relationships with employers, coworkers, friends, and romantic partners that have long-term adverse consequences. We tolerate bad culture in the short term to avoid conflict and earn a paycheck, but the cost to individuals and schools is cynicism that can undermine even the most promising change effort.

Sometimes our anger must extend beyond individual behavior and organizational policies to broader cultural norms. Stanford professor Jennifer L. Eberhardt (2019) is a leading scholar of institutional bias. She tells the story of her five-year-old son, the child of two distinguished African American professionals, who one might think was raised without the tiniest bit of bias or racial insensitivity. As Professor Eberhardt and her son took their seats on a plane, an African American man walked down the aisle, and her son turned to her and said, "I hope that man doesn't rob the plane" (Eberhardt, 2019, p. 3). However jarring, offensive, and embarrassing such a remark might have been, getting angry at her son about being a racist would not have been a particularly constructive reaction. Her anger, rather, has been channeled through her scholarship and advocacy, encompassing audiences from police officers who face the choice of how and when to use deadly force, to employers who consider alternative candidates for hiring and promotion, to teachers who daily react to students' flatteries and provocations. If her own son reflects the biases of our culture, then why should any of us think that, however noble our intentions, we are exempt from societal and cultural influences?

While it may be tempting to be angry with students who appear to be lazy and disengaged, it is more helpful to be angry with the conditions that lead to their disengagement—boredom, distraction, preoccupation with family pathology, bullying, and a host of other factors that, in students' minds, are a bit more important than the homework problems at hand. Change leaders are angry—indeed, they must be angry—but their anger must be directed carefully toward the behaviors, conditions, and cultural influences that are at the heart of the institutions and individuals they wish to change.

CONCLUSION

In the imagining phase of deep change, passion is a necessary but insufficient basis for individual and organizational change. The aspiring change leader who has only directionless passion and lacks the competence and skill to plan and execute change will spend that passionate energy in a futile flameout. Passion with a purpose requires that we are clearheaded about our aspirations as well as the specific things we wish to change. Because change is so difficult, evidence and planning are not enough. We must be angry, and our anger must be carefully directed at the specific behaviors and conditions we wish to change.

REFLECTION

Review the following prompts, and record your responses someplace where you can easily refer to them throughout the deep change journey.

1. Consider a personal or school change that you would like to make now. Imagine the future one year, three years, and five years from now if you are successful in implementing the change. Use as many senses as you can, imagining what you see, hear, and feel. The more vivid your language, the more detailed your vision of the future.
2. Now imagine the future one, three, and five years from now if you do not make the change. Will conditions remain stable? Will they get worse? Using vivid imagery, describe what you see, hear, and feel about this future without change. Does this image generate negative emotions, including anger and impatience? Take a moment to think about those emotions and describe them.
3. Weigh on an imaginary scale these two contrasting images. How does the anger and impatience associated with the failure to change compare to the vivid image of the hopeful future associated with change?

Chapter 7

Focusing

In this chapter, we consider one of the most important elements of deep change leadership: focus. When faced with the need to change, there is an understandable impulse to change everything at once. In our zeal to become more healthy, we will quit smoking (except the occasional legal vape) and drinking (except for the allowable red wine rations), cut the carbohydrates (but not the good kind), cut out red meat (wait—isn't protein supposed to be good now?), stop toxic relationships (except for calls to Mom), avoid the sun (except the good kind of light rays that are way more expensive than natural sunlight), and pursue every other bit of self-help advice that we have squirreled away for another round of New Year's resolutions that will have the life expectancy of a fruit fly. Similarly, when organizational leaders impose strategic plans with hundreds of goals, objectives, and action plans, and after the obligatory investments in pep rallies, consultants, and binders and gigabytes full of directives and strategies . . . nothing happens.

In this chapter, we consider the lure of fragmentation, the costs of fragmentation, the rule of six priorities, and—although focus is essential for leadership success—the costs of focus, or the fear of missing out on the new, new thing. But if effective change is the goal, then focus, not fragmentation or chasing the hot idea of the moment, is required.

THE LURE OF FRAGMENTATION

Educational leaders often pride themselves on being inclusive. They want all stakeholders to have a seat at the table, especially when engaging in long-term planning and setting major goals for schools and districts. Governing board members, parent groups, unions, student activists, local businesses, politicians, and many others have helpful ideas to improve schools. The result of these well-intentioned efforts for inclusiveness is a process of identifying a variety of goals, almost all of which, in isolation, would be worthy of pursuit. For each goal, there are objectives, milestones, and action plans. Soon, the worthy goal is buried under a pile of equally worthy goals, all of which are competing for time and resources. Worse yet, all the new goals are on top of the goals, plans, objectives, and action steps from the previous planning process. The outcome is inevitable fragmentation. Even the most laudable goals—student achievement, equity, and technology access, to name just a few—might have benefited from focused leadership. But as focus yields to fragmentation, the best are buried. Consider one of the most promising practices in education: professional learning communities. While the late Richard DuFour and I (2016) were enthusiastic advocates of the practice, we observed the common state of affairs—what we termed *PLC Lite*, in which carefully planned schedules intended to provide time for teacher collaboration were fragmented because of many other competing demands for the same minutes.

Fragmentation is also the result of the leadership impulse to have the latest and best support for students. This impulse to support students is admirable, but I have never seen a booth at a convention of educational administrators or board members titled "Here Are Things You Can Stop Doing." Instead, the impulse is that if there is better technology, they think, let's buy it. Innovative ideas for personnel management—let's buy them. Innovative ideas for curriculum in schools—let's buy them. All these decisions are based on a sales pitch that claims to be *research based* because, in a different context, the technology, management systems, curriculum, and assessment techniques all work. But the context in which they work is one far more focused and controlled than the context in which the purchasers of those programs live. It's like buying rice cakes from someone who claims that these foods work weight-loss miracles, and then placing the rice cakes on top of a hot fudge sundae after a meal of cheeseburgers and french fries. The purchaser subsequently decides that the rice-cake diet just doesn't work.

Even in the best of circumstances, new ideas gain their momentum under controlled conditions. The new literacy and mathematics program in schools worked well in isolation and in an environment in which this innovation was the primary focus of the school. Leaders made it a priority, and those responsible for implementing it received extensive training and support. But in the real world, innovations are almost never implemented in isolation.

This is the reason that educational innovations that worked so well in the laboratory or carefully controlled classroom often fail in the messy real-world environments in which they are implemented. The challenge is analogous to many medical interventions, such as prescription drugs, which work splendidly when taken as directed. But real patients are notoriously noncompliant in taking prescriptions as directed, as Neil Chesanow (2014) documents in "Why Are So Many Patients Noncompliant?" More than half of the 3.8 billion prescriptions written in the United States every year are taken either incorrectly or not at all. Failure to take medication as directed is associated with as much as 69 percent of hospital admissions and 40 percent of nursing home admissions. If people will not follow directions when their own health is at stake, what makes us think that they will follow the latest directive from the curriculum department or, for that matter, from the superintendent's office? In sum, what matters is not the brilliance or quality of the innovation but the ability of the educators and school administrators to actually implement the innovation.

THE COSTS OF FRAGMENTATION

Greg McKeown (2014) reminds us that the word *priority* came into the English language in about the year 1400 and remained a singular term—meaning the one item that was prior or first among all others. Only in the 20th century did the term become pluralized, as we engaged in the fantasy that setting many priorities made us more productive. According to writer Jory MacKay (2019), the delusion of multiple priorities is directly related to the myth of multitasking and the conviction that, with our 21st century digital minds, we can concentrate on more than one thing at once. While the evidence is clear that humans don't multitask but simply switch from one task to another, the rejoinder that I have heard is that 21st century children are digital natives, with their brains wired differently than those of their analog parents. This claim is unsubstantiated. First, unless we're talking about finches, changes in brain structures take place over tens of thousands of years and many generations, never in a single generation. Second, many experiments about multitasking, including those with very technologically sophisticated MIT and Stanford students, prove conclusively that when students attempt to concentrate on two things at once, their performance diminishes (Crenshaw, 2008; Turkle, 2015). In a series of experiments conducted by Clifford Nass at

Stanford, he confronted his students with the evidence that their performance was reduced when they engaged in multitasking, and the students patiently explained to him that these research findings obviously applied to everyone else but not to them. They were, as they had been raised to believe, exceptional. But they are not. Individuals and organizations perform best when focused, not fragmented.

Fragmentation has a measurably adverse impact on organizational results. For example, in a study I conducted of more than two thousand school plans, I evaluated the relationship between the number of priorities educational leaders attempted to implement and their gains or losses in student achievement over three years (Reeves, 2016). The analysis included students in elementary, middle, and high school grades and all academic disciplines, including literacy, mathematics, science, and social studies. The results were dramatic. Schools with six or fewer priorities had dramatically higher gains than those with more initiatives. Indeed, my colleagues and I found individual schools with more than 70 priorities and education systems with more than 240 priorities (Reeves, 2016). The conclusion was striking: more than six priorities was inversely proportional to gains in performance. The first few priorities allow for focus by leaders, employees, and the entire organization. But after six priorities, it becomes impossible to monitor implementation, and both leaders and employees lose focus.

THE RULE OF SIX

It turns out that the rule of six is not limited to educational organizations; it represents a broadly based human phenomenon. In successful organizations, from Microsoft to complex health-care systems, from the U.S. Army to schools, from universities to global nonprofit organizations, there is a consistent focus on six or fewer priorities. While six may or may not be the magic number, the point is that leaders cannot effectively monitor on a consistent basis the implementation and impact of more than a few initiatives. Many educational leaders maintain a dashboard of key indicators—attendance, safety, achievement, teacher qualifications, and so on. But merely focusing on these effect indicators without also monitoring the causes—the measurable actions of teachers and school leaders that are related to those indicators—can lead to unfortunate consequences. One obvious distortion of actions based on a focus on effect data is cheating. But other distortions are subtler. For example, if test scores are reported only in grades 3–8, then there is little incentive for a school administrator to put highly effective teachers in kindergarten or first grade because, after all, the performance of students in those grades is invisible in the accountability system. In high school, parents are understandably enthusiastic about student performance in Advanced Placement and other college-level classes. But the unintended emphasis on those scores can lead faculty and administrators to restrict access to those classes. Dean R. Spitzer (2019) details how measurements ranging from chicken delivery to automobile manufacturing can cause employees to narrowly pursue the indicator being measured at the expense of the organization's health. The same is true when school measurement of test scores leads to cheating and mindless test preparation rather than effective teaching. In the most shocking example of the unintended consequences of measurement I have personally witnessed, the superintendent made it very clear that attendance was the most important goal, and publicly berated principals with subpar attendance rates. A focus on that key indicator—daily attendance—could have resulted in a redoubled effort to contact students, build relationships with families, and provide transportation and other support in order to get students to school. Or it could have resulted in administrators removing absent students from the enrollment roster. When 400 of 600 students are attending, the rate is a miserable 66 percent. When the same 400 students are attending out of the newly established student population of 440 students, then the attendance rate miraculously rises to 91 percent. The educational and community consequences of removing students from the school roster are dire, but the short-term reward of avoiding the wrath of the superintendent offers an immediate reward for bad decisions. In sum, it's easy to measure test scores and attendance. It's much harder to measure effective teaching and leadership.

THE COSTS OF FOCUS

Although it should be evident that focus is related to student and school success, the lure of fragmentation is a constant threat to successful focus. The same leader who extols the virtues of focus will attend a leadership conference and come back brimming with hot new ideas that must be implemented immediately to keep up with the competition. Teachers who grouse about the multiple fragmented priorities of their principal will cling to personal habits and practices that were long ago rendered useless—think of the pervasive use of word searches—but provide a bit of comfort and familiarity in an environment that is changing with uncomfortable speed. Take a look at your smartphone. Unless you have recently undergone an app cleanse (Siegler, 2015), chances are that you have page after page of smartphone applications, all of which seemed like good ideas when you downloaded them but the vast majority of which have not been used for months or years. Because we desire to be up to date, we strike at every promising new application and device, some of which are ironically promising to save us time, and quickly grow tired of them. Focus is hard. Just ask some children you know about the idea of focusing on fewer gifts that they will play with for longer, and you will instantly become the least favorite adult in their lives. But the same is true of all of us. Decoupling from activities, tools, habits, and devices is profoundly difficult but absolutely necessary if we are to achieve the focus that is imperative for change.

CONCLUSION

Fragmentation is fun. It provides an endless supply of stimulation, like new monsters to kill in a video game, new food in the buffet line, or new dramas, YouTube videos, or other diversions. But fragmentation carries heavy costs for leaders and the schools and districts they serve. The huge gap between promise and reality is due to the dramatic differences between the conditions under which promising initiatives are tested and the realistic conditions under which they are delivered. Evidence strongly suggests that when leaders have more than six priorities, they lose focus or tend to measure their progress ineffectively. Focus, however beneficial, has costs. Colleagues who advocate for the *new thing* will be disappointed when the leader does not readily grasp for the latest curriculum, data-analysis program, or workshop. Leaders themselves may fear that they will miss out on innovations that competing schools have implemented. And most of all, the embrace of promising new practices requires the deliberate abandonment of old practices, a process that is painful and full of separation anxiety.

REFLECTION

Review the following prompts, and record your responses someplace where you can easily refer to them throughout the deep change journey.

1. Take an inventory of the priorities for your district and for your school. Consider not only the official priorities as reflected in school improvement plans, strategic plans, and other official documents but also the unofficial priorities based on what teachers and school administrators actually do. It will be very helpful to make this a clear and visible list.
2. After you have made the list, ask classroom educators and building principals whether you missed anything. Every time I have tried this

reflective exercise, I find that the list of priorities is much longer when I ask people closest to the students to list them.

3. For each priority, identify the source. Is it a current requirement? Is it something required by previous administrators? Is it state or local policy? Because there are almost always more priorities than teachers and leaders have time to implement, identifying the source will help to address the claim that "we have to do this because it's required."

Chapter 8

Implementing

Implementation is a leadership discipline. It's about getting things done with responsible individuals, teams, and the entire school and educational system. The implementing phase of deep change makes clear the frailty of the traditional leadership and management dichotomy. One cannot be an effective leader without the management disciplines inherent in implementation, and in this chapter, we will explore those disciplines. This chapter will focus on creating leading indicators and maintaining a culture of accountability.

LEADING INDICATORS

The importance of leading indicators is illustrated in figure 8.1 (page 84), the leadership and learning matrix. The vertical axis represents results, and the horizontal axis represents causes—what I call here the *antecedents of excellence*. The central implication of the matrix is that with a deep understanding of both results and causes, leaders will be able to make better, sounder decisions based on personal and organizational learning rather than gut instinct.

Lucky	Leading
High results, low understanding of antecedents Replication of success unlikely	High results, high understanding of antecedents Replication of success likely
Losing	**Learning**
Low results, low understanding of antecedents D'oh!	Low results, high understanding of antecedents Replication of success likely

ACHIEVEMENT OF RESULTS

CAUSES: THE ANTECEDENTS OF EXCELLENCE

Source: Reeves, 2002. Used with permission.

FIGURE 8.1: The leadership and learning matrix.

In the lower-left-hand quadrant are the losing leaders. These are the spectacularly ineffective leaders who not only are failing but don't understand the reason for their failures. These are the principals who, for many years, have watched students fail in literacy performance but maintain the same schedule, curriculum, assessment, and teaching practices. They continue to do the same thing while hoping for different results.

The upper-left-hand quadrant, featuring the lucky leaders, represents the schools in which students begin with substantial advantages that, as a result, make the accountability measures look great. This is typical of elite schools—public and private—that are selective in accepting students. If, for example, a school excludes students with poor literacy and mathematics skills, poor attendance, and inadequate parental support, then it does not require federally funded research to confirm that this school sees good results in literacy and mathematics, great attendance, and marvelous parental support. This has nothing to do with leadership and everything to do with selection—the leaders of these schools are more lucky than skillful.

The lower-right-hand quadrant, with the learning leaders, represents great promise. These are the leaders who have the greatest potential to transform deep change into student results. These leaders face enormous difficulties—results are down, layoffs may be necessary, restructuring is required—yet because they are on the right side of the matrix, they demonstrate a deep understanding of the causes of success and, eventually, how to replicate those causes and achieve success. But boards of education and voters are notoriously impatient with the learning leader. Consider the previous examples of Presidents Johnson and Nixon, both of whom went from overwhelming victories to defeats—Johnson by declining to run and Nixon by resigning—in just a few years. Business case studies look at the house of cards on which Enron was built, and students exclaim, "Of course they were corrupt and unsustainable!" while not recognizing that the company, shortly before its bankruptcy, graced the pages of prestigious business journals and books. There are tragic examples of school and district leaders who were heralded in the news and recognized for their success but who later were discredited because of cheating scandals.

Learning leaders look like losing leaders if all you consider are the results. Learning leaders exemplify the persistence of the Stoics (Irvine, 2019). Like Seneca of ancient times, modern stoics are relentless learners, using every setback as a lesson and source of encouragement. Abraham Lincoln famously lost one election after the other before ultimately achieving the highest office in the land and becoming, by the account of many historians, the greatest leader in U.S. history, saving the nation in its darkest hour. According to writer and editor Emily Temple (2017), Madeleine L'Engle's *A Wrinkle in Time* was rejected by 26 publishers, and Robert M. Pirsig's *Zen and the Art of Motorcycle Maintenance* was rejected by 121 publishers before its ultimate and enduring success. My literary career began with my sending faxes, in the days when a fax connoted a sense of urgency and importance, to two hundred literary agents. Two responded, one in New York and one in Boston. The New York trip resulted in failure. The Boston trip resulted in a relationship with Esmond Harmsworth, one of the world's best agents. That relationship started with a three-book contract with a major publisher and continues two decades later. Had I given up after a few rejections, or even after one hundred rejections, I would never have found Esmond and would never have published forty-one books.

In the upper-right-hand quadrant are the leading leaders, those who have both great results and an understanding of how they achieved them. These are the deep change leaders. But how does a leader arrive in this quadrant? A very few may take the helm when an organization is already successful, they understand the basis of this success, and their mandate from the governing boards is, "Please—just don't mess it up!" But in my interviews with leaders who have earned this designation in the upper-right-hand quadrant, I have never found one whose path to success was smooth. They learned from mistakes and endured the humiliating process of admitting those mistakes. This stands in stark contrast to the losing and lucky leaders, who are often wrong but never in doubt. The path to the leading quadrant is paved not only with mistakes but with the quest for understanding. For these leaders, it is not enough to be accountable for results. Rather, accountability must be a learning system that, as the leadership and learning matrix suggests, integrates results with a deep understanding of the antecedents of excellence.

ACCOUNTABILITY AS A LEARNING SYSTEM

Consider the phrase, "We're going to hold you accountable." What emotions does that provoke? I strongly suspect that, in most organizations, it is not a phrase that engenders the response, "Hold me accountable? That's great news! I can't wait, because every time someone has held me accountable, I always learned something of value." When it comes to accountability, leaders face two starkly different choices. One is that they can pursue the traditional form of accountability in which a school administrator, endowed with mystical insights associated with his or her title, judges the work of others, often using instruments that have the illusion of precision but are in fact full of ambiguity and error (Buckingham & Goodall, 2019). The worst accountability systems consider not the objective achievements of individuals and teams but comparisons that pit one colleague against another, undermining collaboration and trust (Edmondson, 2019). In education, one of the worst examples of this sort of toxic accountability is when there is a limited bonus pool that administrators must allocate to the "best" teachers, insuring that collaboration is undermined. Worse yet, these teachers, who are expected to operate in a standards-based environment, are judged in a norm-based environment. "Don't you dare use the bell curve to evaluate students," they are told, while administrators use the bell curve to compare teachers to one another. The other choice is accountability as a learning system. Rather than rely on ratings bestowed from one level of the hierarchy to the next, accountability as a learning system requires leaders to consider not only results but causes. Return to figure 8.1 (page 84), and focus on the vertical axis—results. When accountability systems fixate only on this axis, leaders cannot distinguish between the losing leader and the learning leader, as they both have low results. Because the results look good in the top two quadrants, leaders cannot distinguish between the lucky leader and the leading leader. This risk-rewarding performance may or may not be the result of effective leadership. A learning system, by contrast, considers both the vertical and horizontal axes. Two teams or individuals could have identical results, but a consideration of the causes—the antecedents of excellence—allows leaders to gain insights that are beyond the scope of the typical dashboard. When schools are redistricted, the student population changes—and sometimes the results along with it—but the faculty and leadership remain the same. Were those changes due to the skill or failures of the faculty and leader or the changes in school boundaries? When the state engages a new vendor for the spring test, scores often go down, not because teachers are incompetent but because the new test is unfamiliar in format and content. When accountability focuses on learning rather than blame, we can detect the critical underlying causes.

CONCLUSION

The value of leading indicators is that leaders will receive feedback on what is going well and what needs improvement before it is too late to address root causes. When change leaders do this, they will have built accountability as a learning system.

REFLECTION

Review the following prompts, and record your responses someplace where you can easily refer to them throughout the deep change journey.

1. What are your one or two wildly important goals?
2. Reflecting on your present level of progress, which quadrant are you in—lucky, losing, learning, or leading? What are one or two leadership actions that you can take to proceed to another quadrant?
3. What is a leading indicator for one of your wildly important goals?
4. What are the barriers to your goal that you can remove right now?

Chapter 9

Accelerating

This is the essence of deep change: imagining, focusing, implementing, and accelerating. Imagining requires both positive and negative visions that are, respectively, compelling and repellent. Focusing requires leaders to be intensively clear not only about the goals that they pursue but also about what they will not do. Implementing involves the teachers' and educational administrators' observable actions being part of the daily rhythm of accountability for schools. Now we turn our attention to accelerating—dramatically changing the pace of change from traditional five-year plans to immediate impact. In this chapter, we will consider the elements of accelerating. In contrast to multiyear strategic plans, accelerating requires a focus on short-cycle feedback, typically ranging from six weeks to one hundred days. Rather than focusing on end-of-year test scores, we focus on measuring what matters. These short-cycle measurements allow faculty and staff to celebrate meaningful progress.

PROVIDE SHORT-CYCLE FEEDBACK

In *100-Day Leaders,* Robert Eaker and I (2019) argue that extraordinary things can be accomplished in one hundred days. John Hattie (2012) demonstrates that educational innovations can be tested and evaluated in as few as six weeks. In many ways, it is the perfect experiment, as the students are identical—as are the teacher, schedule, funding, nutrition, and other variables that can often distort educational research. We can measure student performance before an intervention and six weeks later measure the progress or lack of it. This provides a cycle of continuous learning in which educators can experiment with innovative practices and evaluate them immediately. Student progress, especially in skill development, such as reading, mathematics, and personal organization, can be objectively measured in this way. It's the same reason that athletic coaches review game films, making appropriate adjustments and seeing what works and what doesn't on a week-to-week basis.

One of the reasons that deep change leaders need short-cycle feedback is that schools in need of deep change have often been beat down, humiliated, and labeled. These schools, labeled with terms like *academic distress* and—my favorite—*schools in need of improvement* (or *SIN* schools, as they are known), labor under conditions that threaten staff and undermine morale. Staff don't need a five-year plan or next year's test results to validate their work. They need to know that, as a result of their dedication and hard work, they can gain some recognition and respect. As schools endured shutdowns during the pandemic of 2020, it was not unusual to see record numbers of student failures. These failures were often associated with policies that required, for example, a student with ten unexcused absences to fail the class. Incredibly, this pre-pandemic policy applied even to students who missed classes because of lack of computers and lack of connectivity. This has led to a national crisis that I call the *dropout time bomb*, which will have lingering effects long after 2020 (Reeves, 2020b). The good news is that the dropout time bomb can be defused. For example, when schools make deliberate policy decisions to calculate the final semester grade based on student performance at the time the grade is awarded, rather than the average of student performance throughout the semester, the number of failures drops dramatically. Even in the midst of a crisis, teachers and schools can achieve short-cycle success by comparing failure rates in the first quarter of a semester to the final semester grades, and celebrate a significant and profound impact on student results. Without the positive reinforcement associated with short-cycle results, schools suffer a malaise in which teachers' shared belief system changes from "We make a difference!" to "There's nothing we can do." One of the most important roles of deep change leaders is to reinforce continuously the evidence-backed belief that teachers and school leaders really do make a difference for students.

MEASURE WHAT MATTERS

Stephen Jay Gould's (1981, 2008) *The Mismeasure of Man* should be required reading for every leader. It chronicles the collective folly of scholars and politicians who, for their own motives, seek to extol the virtues of biological determinism. Decades after its initial publication, the book remains a pillar of discourse that is rational, elegant, and, most importantly, based on evidence rather than popularity. Although the focus of Gould's argument has to do with the use of intelligence tests as a singular measurement of human potential and success, the broader arguments that it provides are essential for every change leader.

First, measure what is important, not what is easy to measure. Convenience, as Gould (2008) argues, is not necessarily correct. It is easy, for example, to measure the bumps on a head or the cranial capacity of a skull, though the former measurement is easier for a living subject and the latter more convenient for a dead one. Measuring characteristics such as adaptability, resistance, collegiality, and spite are more challenging, regardless of which side of the River Styx the subject resides on. Leaders often seek to measure potential rather than performance, but that is a fool's errand (Buckingham & Goodall, 2019). The best we can do is observe and measure truth—the square of the hypotenuse is, at least on a perfect plane, equal to the sum of the square of the two sides. That's not the same as predicting that Pythagoras and his children will be particularly effective mathematicians. In schools, leaders must decide to measure what teachers and students actually do, not just what they say. I can measure, for example, the percentage of students in a classroom who are engaged in the lesson. I can measure the percentage of classrooms in which teachers call on students randomly to insure equity rather than wait for the usual volunteers to raise their hands. I can measure the percentage of students who can tell me what they are learning and what will happen next. These are not the mystical observations of a connoisseur but objective truth.

Second, admit what cannot be measured. We can measure the percentage of answers to questions that a test taker selects that are identical to the answers that the test writer defined as correct. That is not at all the same as measuring the percentage of correct answers, a distinction that continues to elude examiners from the testing behemoths to supremely confident teachers, as well as erudite professors who are willing to acknowledge only a single correct response. To put a fine point on it, we can measure students' SAT scores or, a few years earlier, students' scores on the admissions tests for the competitive public and private schools in Boston and New York. Boston Latin School, the oldest public school in the United States, will celebrate its four hundredth anniversary in 2035. I've been there, and it's a fine place, full of great teachers and a wide variety of extracurricular activities. But if a school accepts only the top 1 percent of students, then, like Bronx High School of Science or any number of other highly selective public and private schools, the students will do quite well. As network scientist Albert-László Barabási (2018) concludes, in a highly selective system, it is not the school that makes the student but the student who makes the school. The admissions tests measure putatively correct answers. They also reflect the ambition, parental involvement, and executive function skills that led to the high test scores.

Third, classify falsehoods as falsehoods, not as scholarly disagreements. Gould (2008) reminds us that distinguished scientists could "prove," with scientific evidence, that Irish, Italians, Slavs, Chinese, and Africans were inferior. These arguments were not a matter of scholarly debate but, in the most accurate prose possible, damned lies. Gould (2008) and the many scholars he cites are manifestly modest about admitting what they know and what they do not know. Gould's colleague Howard Gardner (2011), as discussed in chapter 1 (page 15), offers the theory of multiple intelligences not as settled science but as a theory to be tested in the caldron of experimentation. Real scholars ask for evidence; false scholars fear it. Gould (2008) brilliantly distinguishes the arguments of *The Bell Curve* (Herrnstein & Murray, 1994) as academic disagreements, misunderstandings of data, and outright lies. Change leaders must frequently confront the same challenges Gould faces.

Consider an example in which the scores of fourth-grade students on a state literacy test improve from one year to the other. The publisher who sold the literacy program attributes this success to great textbooks, the teachers attribute the success to great instruction, and the parents attribute success to terrific parenting. Behavior improves in a school because of an effective discipline program, improved relationships with teachers, or simply the fact that administrators stopped accepting discipline referrals. In brief, life is multivariate—there is always more than one cause for any effect.

Fourth, don't avoid the hard stuff—the more complex analysis of the relationship between causes and effects. Once we acknowledge that life is multivariate, we must also accept that we need to engage in analysis that extends beyond the middle school mathematics of *x*-*y* graphs, in which the *x* (horizontal) axis represents the cause variables and the *y* (vertical) axis represents the effects. This sort of analysis is a starting point but certainly not the ending point of understanding the many causes of a single effect.

CELEBRATE MEANINGFUL PROGRESS

Now that we know that meaningful measurement can be done, the question is what to do with those results. And the answer is *celebrate*. Deep change leaders do not let a day go by without meaningful celebrations. Let me illustrate with two examples from opposite ends of the grade spectrum.

Student writing—especially nonfiction writing intended to describe, compare, evaluate, and persuade—has been strongly linked to improved student achievement in every discipline (Reeves, 2020a). As I know from working with them directly, kindergarten teachers in Lima, Ohio, are deeply committed to improving literacy for the students in their high-poverty system. At Unity Elementary School, teachers Desiray Engberg and Jessica Griffith, instructional coach Amber Vernon, and principal Tricia Winkler brilliantly created a range of fifteen levels of student writing, all described in student language, and captured on video students describing how they could get to the next level. Whenever I see evidence of great student performance like this, it makes me intolerant of anyone who claims that writing for kindergarteners is developmentally inappropriate. These students love being successful, showing progress day by day in their classes. They don't need end-of-year state test scores to validate their success, but they can celebrate every day their progress, which teachers have carefully orchestrated along a continuum.

Similarly, at Lima Senior High School, a beacon of hope in an area beset by violence, poverty, homelessness, and family trauma, teachers Chrissy Hood and Melissa Donald had their entrepreneurship class create a wax museum in which each student impersonated an entrepreneurial mentor. Students' enthusiastic choices ranged from Madam C. J. Walker, the first African American woman millionaire, who pioneered beauty products in the early 20th century and whose products continue to be used well into the 21st century, to sports and entertainment figures. What was particularly noteworthy about these thoughtful and articulate students' displays was that they included not only entrepreneurs' business and financial success but their commitments to community service and charity. Teachers created brilliant scoring rubrics, helping students of every ability level build their displays at their own pace.

In both of these cases, the cycle of assessment was immediate. Students could leave every class knowing that they were making progress and, impressively, explain to visitors exactly how they were making progress toward their goals. Contrast that with classes in which the primary—and sometimes the only—measurement of student progress is a single exam at the end of a unit, quarter, or semester.

The more frequent the feedback, the more likely that students and teachers can use that feedback to adjust learning strategies and get back on track to success.

CONCLUSION

Accelerating deep change provides the emotional and organizational momentum that is necessary for every school. Acceleration is much different from the more common ethic expressed in the statement, "Thank goodness that change initiative is over—now we can go back to what we were doing before." In deep change, implementation gets faster and more effective. In part 3, we move from these ideas to further action.

REFLECTION

Review the following prompts, and record your responses someplace where you can easily refer to them throughout the deep change journey.

1. Which classes, programs, or extracurricular activities in your school or district practice the disciplines involved in accelerating? That is, which offer short-cycle feedback for continuous student improvement? Identify those in which progress is objectively measured and students are able to monitor and explain their own progress toward their performance goals. What trends do you see in these examples of accelerating?
2. How could you apply the principles of accelerating to faculty and administrators in your school or district? For example, how could feedback about staff meetings, professional learning, and grade-level meetings be provided and monitored so that professionals in your school or district know that their performance is improving every day?

PART 3

THE PATH AHEAD

At the beginning of this book, we considered the evidence that the vast majority of change efforts fail. In the next several chapters, we will consider how change leaders can make course corrections, avoid the predictable mistakes that affect most change efforts, and build a team of change leaders. While change leadership can feel like a solitary endeavor, it need not be that way. Change leaders need the organizational and emotional support of one another in order to see their vision of change become a reality.

Chapter 10

Making Course Corrections

Business-growth expert Scott Duffy (2018) compares leadership decisions to landing a high-performance jet on the deck of an aircraft carrier. The flight deck is not only much narrower and shorter than a land-based runway, but it is also moving—side to side and up and down—making a landing especially complex and precarious. There are three options for such a landing. Ideally, the pilot deploys a hook, which snags a heavy line on the deck, and the aircraft is pulled to an abrupt stop. If the hook misses, however, the pilot has only two seconds to accelerate and take off for another landing attempt. If the acceleration is not sufficient or the pilot's reactions are a second too slow, then the aircraft falls off the end of the carrier and plunges into the water. Even the most experienced pilots miss the landing and require multiple attempts to safely land the jet. For them, course corrections are not an exceptional reaction to an error but part of their daily lives.

All pilots—whether flying military aircraft, commercial jets, or propeller planes—have a flight plan, and they know that the flight plan is simply where they start a flight. But wind conditions and other factors require not merely following the flight plan but making constant adjustments throughout the flight, comparing the actual position of the aircraft to the position that is necessary to reach the destination. Thus, the successful pilot of an aircraft is responding to a continuous flow of information so that he or she can make the changes necessary for a safe and successful mission.

As I argued earlier in this book, the folly of many strategic plans is that they assume a consistent environment and a level of consistent execution of plans and pursuit of goals without acknowledging that the environment is constantly changing. A plan that does not anticipate these changes and consider how leaders and organizations must respond quickly to those changes puts the organization at risk and makes the plan look ridiculous. Consider the relevance of strategic plans crafted in January 2020. When, weeks later, schools were closed, staff members were ill, students were idle, and parents were frantic, how relevant was the five-year plan?

To learn how to become skilled at making course corrections, we must explore the essential nature of errors, decision disciplines, and what it means to be an agile leader.

THE ESSENTIAL NATURE OF ERRORS

It's embarrassing to make errors. Some leaders think it's even more embarrassing to admit errors, so they inexplicably persist in the pursuit of failed strategies, even as conditions change and a steady stream of information screams for a change in direction. London Business School professors Freek Vermeulen and Niro Sivanathan (2017) note that this bullheaded resistance to acknowledging errors costs billions of dollars and untold human misery as organizations fail, employees lose jobs, and families are devastated. If you are not persuaded of the essential nature of errors, and of admitting those errors frequently, consider that San Francisco Conservatory of Music professor and award-winning composer Robert Greenberg (n.d.) loves to play some of the early drafts of Beethoven's iconic Fifth Symphony, the first few notes of which even the most musically impaired person will recognize—da, da, da, *dum*. These notes are not only famous musically but widely recognized as the Morse code for *V*—victory—in World War II. But this wonderful symphony didn't have very auspicious beginnings. Greenberg's (n.d.) research reveals early drafts that are amateurish and completely forgettable. We can bask in the glory of the Fifth Symphony and so many other wonderful works because Beethoven was willing to admit errors.

DECISION DISCIPLINES

As in music and art, the advancement of science depends on a relentless search for and admission of error. In their *Harvard Business Review* article on leadership, A. G. Lafley, Roger L. Martin, Jan W. Rivkin, and Nicolaj Siggelkow (2012) advocate for bringing the discipline of science to strategy. Every decision, both in science and in the leadership of organizations, is essentially a hypothesis. The nature of any hypothesis worthy of the name is that it is falsifiable—that is, future evidence will be either consistent or inconsistent with the hypothesis, and when data are inconsistent, scientists and leaders must either articulate a new hypothesis or suppose that the data are irrelevant, insufficient, and inapplicable. Scientists do this reflexively; that is how science has advanced since the Enlightenment. Organizational leaders, by contrast, are too often loath to do so. Why the resistance to alternative hypotheses and what Lafley and colleagues (2012) call "mutually exclusive decision alternatives"? That requires winners and losers, but most social organizations, including businesses, nonprofits, governmental entities, and schools, thrive on consensus. Even when there are vigorous disagreements among staff, by the time a recommendation comes to the leader, it has been sanitized, scrubbed of dissent and doubt, leaving the illusion of a perfect decision, or at least one with a very high probability of success. A far better approach to decision making is the requirement that for every decision, there are at least two mutually exclusive alternatives. Accepting one means rejecting the other. Each alternative has both advantages and disadvantages. If staff claim that there is such a thing as a disadvantage-free decision alternative, they simply have not done their homework.

This commitment to decision discipline requires a mindset change. Good, thoughtful leaders and teachers will advocate a decision, and it will be rejected. That does not imply rejection of them as people or leaders. They serve the organization well by engaging in a disciplined process, and it is the process, not personal or turf victories, that is essential. Schools have a fixed amount of time, and therefore teachers and administrators face mutually exclusive decisions daily: Do I teach the lesson on the pacing guide or reteach key concepts that my students don't understand? Do I devote the faculty meeting to announcements and news updates, or do I devote that time to allowing teachers to create common formative assessments? Do I provide an additional literacy course for students who are below grade level in reading, or do I provide a French elective? Unfortunately, many schools are so overloaded with initiatives that they operate under the illusion that they can simultaneously implement many different programs within the same limited number of hours.

The inevitable result is the Law of Initiative Fatigue (Reeves, 2020c); in schools' futile attempt to implement many competing initiatives, none of the initiatives are done well. For example, in a school I visited in 2020, teachers were allowed to choose their distance-learning platform, with some using Zoom, others Webex, others Schoology, and others Google Meet. Each of these platforms has its idiosyncrasies. Imagine a student who, in addition to adapting to a complex distance-learning environment, must also master four different video platforms each day. Similar overload occurs when teachers must administer a blizzard of assessments, including benchmark assessments, formative assessments, unit assessments, and end-of-course assessments. While each of these assessments had a purpose when proposed—the use of assessment data to inform instruction—the cumulative effect of many assessments is the opposite of what leaders intend. Time is a zero-sum game, and every hour devoted to assessment is an hour removed from instruction. Rather than use the data from these assessments, teachers rush through curriculum, fearful that they will not have the time to cover the required curriculum.

There are always at least two candidates for hiring and promotion, at least two alternatives for every investment, and at least two alternatives for software and hardware decisions. These are also the three areas in which there is information asymmetry: a few people have, or claim to have, superior information. In interviews, despite their widely reported unreliability (Peirce, 2017), leaders fall in and out of love with candidates and offer little more than a gut feeling to make very expensive hiring and promotion decisions. Some leaders have greater knowledge about finance and technology, but that does not give them superior insights. If anything, those with greater access to information have a particular obligation to carefully explain the advantages and disadvantages of every alternative. Words that every decision maker should fear are, "What's the matter—don't you trust me?" uttered by those who claim to have special insight. U.S. president Ronald Reagan's maxim "Trust, but verify" applies to leaders today as much as ever (Swaim, 2016). The discipline of mutually exclusive alternatives will have a dramatically positive impact on meetings. Whereas too many meetings are focused on presentation, with the leader expected to make an up-or-down decision, mutually exclusive alternatives will shift the focus of the meeting from presentation to deliberation. That is the best use of meeting time and energy.

The discipline of a consideration of alternatives requires a high tolerance for dissonance among staff. Consider the volatile issues of equity and racism in schools.

As I have followed these discussions on social media, it is more common to find posts that end with exclamation marks than with question marks. If educational organizations are serious about improving equity and addressing racism, it will help if we seek the best solution among many alternatives, not merely the solution that is the loudest and most passionate at any given moment. Leaders must be willing to engage in a concentrated commitment to listening and learning, including listening to diverse voices, before they fall victim to the easiest or fastest solutions to complex challenges.

THE AGILE LEADER

Leading change is difficult enough. Making changes while leading change is even more challenging. The hallmarks of agile leadership are the ability to quickly respond to new information and take decisive action. While educational leaders often resent the suggestion that ideas that work in business apply to education, agile leadership may be a pleasant exception to that rule. If ever there were a leadership position that required agility, it is the school, district, state, and national leader in education. Simon Hayward (2018) has amassed significant evidence that agile leadership has sustainable quantitative advantages. Schools' shift to distance learning worldwide in the spring of 2020 is a dramatic example of the difference that agile leadership makes. The schools that adapted most effectively to the crisis had already taken the initiative to provide computers to every student and staff member, so the change to technology-based learning was faster and more seamless than those schools that began to purchase computers in the midst of the pandemic. But it doesn't take a crisis for agile leadership to succeed. For example, I have seen agile leaders in schools and districts develop and deploy new curricula in a year, a process that used to take three times as long. I've seen mathematics teachers make changes in a single semester, such as moving from traditional homework to solving problems during class, and dramatically reducing the failure rate and improving classroom engagement. But the reason that agile leadership is generally so elusive, Hayward (2018) argues, is that it requires a leader who is simultaneously an enabler and a disrupter, what he describes as the "agile leadership paradox" (p. 3). They must provide stability, reassuring employees, customers, and other stakeholders that the organization is trustworthy and can be relied on during turbulent times, and also be able to make lightning-fast changes when necessary. McKinsey, the global consultancy, finds that only 12 percent of more than one thousand companies it studied exhibited these agile characteristics (Hayward, 2018). Not surprisingly, these companies had better financial and organizational results than their less agile peers. A ten-year study of leadership performance by Elena Lytkina Botelho, Kim Rosenkoetter Powell, Stephen Kincaid, and Dina Wang (2017) finds that leaders who excelled at adapting quickly to changing circumstances were almost seven times more likely to succeed. When leaders failed to adapt, they were likely to be among the 25 percent of leadership departures that were involuntary, a turnover rate that cost shareholders in excess of $100 billion.

How quickly must leaders respond to changing conditions? Standing at the plate, the batter in baseball has only fractions of a second to decide whether to swing, bunt, wait, or, in some cases, duck. The ball is approaching at speeds of nearly one hundred miles per hour, and batters often make the decision about their reaction to the pitch within milliseconds after the ball has left the pitcher's hands. The fastest pitches in another of the world's most popular games, cricket, also exceed one hundred miles per hour. Batters and batsmen, respectively, must react instantly—they are agile in the extreme. The very best traditions of both games require not only exceptional skill but sportsmanship and integrity, team play, and decisive action—precisely the characteristics of agile leaders. Hayward (2018) continues the analogy between leadership agility and physical agility with these five characteristics of exceptional physical agility.

1. Balance
2. Strength
3. Speed
4. Coordination
5. Endurance

Teaching is a physically demanding occupation, and school leaders are wise to pay attention to the needs of classroom educators for physical health as well as pedagogical excellence. A growing number of the schools I observe are embracing opportunities for mindfulness for students, teachers, and leaders, as well as supporting classes in yoga and other practices to reduce stress and improve health.

There is one more athletic analogy that illuminates the characteristics of the agile leader, and that is the role of the coach in Australian rules football, known as *footy*. The game is the oldest form of football in the world, predating the U.S. version by several decades. Footy is a joy to watch. The action is continuous, as there are no time-outs. Coaches cannot stop the game and review films, challenge the ruling of officials, or break for a beer commercial. They just play the game, intensively, competitively, and continuously. U.S. football coaches stride up and down the sidelines gesticulating, sometimes cursing the officials and players, and promising the expectant fans a cardiac event as exciting as two three-hundred-pound players crashing into each other. It appears that they wish they were still playing the game, yearning to make just one more tackle or catch another pass. By contrast, the Australian rules coach must sit in a box far removed from the field of play. The coach can send instructions through runners but otherwise cannot speak to players except for in brief periods before the game and during intervals between periods of play. It's also noteworthy that, unlike its U.S. counterpart, footy has a half million women and girls playing in Australia alone, and women coach at the amateur and professional levels. While agile leaders need not sit in a glass box, it is a metaphor worth considering, as leaders discard the egocentrism that suggests that only they can make the magic happen, when the truth is that sustained organizational excellence and ability require leaders to empower others.

CONCLUSION

In this chapter, we considered the essential nature of errors. Progress and learning are impossible without errors and, most importantly, the prompt and candid admission of those errors. Art, music, and science would remain in primitive states were it not for the ability of the artist, musician, and scientist to admit errors, slash the canvas, burn the manuscript, and change hypotheses in pursuit of greater levels of beauty and truth.

In order to minimize senseless errors, leaders must embrace the most important decision discipline: that of requiring mutually exclusive decision alternatives. This is especially important for high-risk decisions involving people, money, and technology. Moreover, the demand for decision alternatives, with a complete understanding of advantages and disadvantages of each alternative, must be available when information is not easily available. This is especially true in areas like finance and technology, when a few people have access to detailed information that may not be readily available to other leaders. Change leaders live by the maxim "Trust, but verify."

Finally, we considered the characteristics of the agile leader, and we documented the dramatically improved results available to the leader who can resolve the paradox of simultaneously providing disruption and stability in an environment of challenge and encouragement.

REFLECTION

Review the following prompts, and record your responses someplace where you can easily refer to them throughout the deep change journey.

1. What can you do for your own emotional and physical health this week?
2. Consider a decision that you must make in the next few months. It could be about a curriculum, an instructional strategy, a technology implementation, or a hiring decision. As you think this over, it's natural to want to identify the potential advantages and disadvantages of the decision you intend to make. However, based on the decision disciplines we learned in this chapter, record an alternative you could consider. You cannot blend the alternatives—you have to choose among at least two mutually exclusive alternatives. That is, if you adopt an addition to your curriculum, you will be rejecting some curriculum that is now in the schedule. If you adopt a new technology program, then the time devoted to it will inevitably be taken from current technology programs. When you clearly reject one option in order to accept another, what do you notice about your thought process?
3. Think of a change initiative that is in progress right now and is not going as planned. Use what you know about agile leadership to think of midcourse corrections that you and your colleagues can make right now.

Chapter 11

Anticipating Mistakes in Change Leadership

In this chapter, we explore the most common mistakes in change leadership and how to either avoid them or minimize their impact. Despite the high failure rate of change, many organizational leaders persist in doing the same thing and expecting different results. Leaders use mid-20th century practices of long-term strategic plans, participation tactics that look like a New England town meeting of the 17th century, or, more to the point, Athenian democracy more than two millennia ago. It is possible to learn from these mistakes, and the first step is to admit our vulnerability to them.

THE MOST COMMON CHANGE LEADERSHIP MISTAKES

In his seminal work on change leadership, Harvard professor John Kotter (1995) identifies eight reasons that change efforts fail. The sign of a person of integrity—particularly among professors and consultants—is when he or she talks not only about successful engagements but also about failures. Kotter's honesty is a model for us all, a blueprint for change leaders who might be tempted to talk only about the advantages of change without candidly addressing the risks. He notes that organizational-change efforts sometimes are in pursuit of new opportunities but often are in reaction to changes in external conditions that, if left unchecked, might threaten the future of the organization. Thus, a great deal of change is based on fear. He argues that the first mistake in change leadership, and one that leads to many subsequent mistakes, is the failure to create a sufficient sense of urgency for the change. Kotter (1995) estimates that more than half of the companies he has observed entered into change programs without the necessary level of urgency. This occurs because leaders overestimate their own success in creating change and dramatically underestimate organizational resistance. Educational leaders must weigh the urgent nature of a change against inevitable resistance to change. It is common, for example, for a small number of teachers to be responsible for a large number of failures. As superintendent Jill Ackerman told me:

> When the same students are getting As and Bs in some classes and failing other classes, that's a teaching problem. The students are showing up, but, in some classes, they have positive relationships with teachers and, in other classes, they don't. It's up to us to address that. (J. Ackerman, personal communication, October 27, 2020)

Excessive student failures can cascade into a dropout crisis (Reeves, 2020b). It is possible to prevent failures and dropouts, but it requires leaders' decisive action and willingness to endure resistance and criticism.

Kotter (1995) is the creator of the *guiding coalition* to lead change. The second mistake that many organizations make, however, is understanding the word *coalition* to mean something like a legislative body that represents all stakeholders (Kotter, 1995). This is a prescription for paralysis. I have seen small school systems with more than one hundred people involved in their planning processes. Rather than focus on the needs of the entire district, large groups tend to represent their constituencies, and what starts as a coherent change process breaks down into every stakeholder defending resources and positions. The objective of any serious change effort is not placating every interested party, because the only way to do that is to avoid change. Meaningful change will inevitably involve reallocation of resources and leadership attention to support the most important elements of the change vision. Attempting to spread the wealth in terms of representation on the coalition will place the change effort in mortal peril, and the problem is compounded when the seats on the coalition are delegated to staff positions, such as planning and analysis. Kotter (1995) rightly insists that the coalition must have senior line leaders—a relatively small number of people with responsibility for results—or else the coalition will dissolve into turf wars in which the objective is no longer the pursuit of the change vision but the protection of parochial interests. Edmondson (2019) adds some nuance to the consideration of guiding coalitions. Change leaders must be inclusive enough to show genuine interest in the views of others, but not inadvertently send the signal that everyone gets to vote on every change. She suggests that changes can be differentiated by a culture of telling, in which leaders simply explain their vision and expect others to follow, and a culture of inquiry, in which leaders express genuine interest in others. She calls these sort of conversations "purposeful probing" so that leaders dig beneath the surface-level responses in which people might be tempted to simply say what they think the boss wants to hear, and truly understand the emotions; backgrounds; fears; and, most importantly, hopes of all team members (Edmondson, 2019, p. 170).

A third mistake is the use of anemic, unclear, or one-dimensional visions for change (Kotter, 1995). For example, if the only vision is *increasing stakeholder engagement*, then it potentially leaves the interests of students and staff out of the picture. And many vision statements that I have seen are evidently the work of a committee, with one vague platitude stitched to the next. Just as most strategic plans fall apart under the weight of initiative fatigue, ineffective change visions can be buried under a pile of programs and objectives that are not coherently connected. Note, too, that change leaders have colleagues from different cultural backgrounds, often speaking different languages, with widely varying perspectives. It's imperative that leaders produce a crystal-clear vision for change.

The fourth mistake Kotter (1995) identifies is the failure to communicate the vision. He suggests that leaders calculate the total amount of communication that happens in an organization—meetings, emails, seminars, and so on. According to research from the consulting firm Bain & Company, that quantity has risen dramatically every year since 2008 (Mankins & Garton, 2017). Kotter (1995) then challenges us to divide the amount of communication about the change vision by the total amount of communication in the organization. His estimate is that communication of the vision captures only 0.0005 percent of total communication, yet leaders seem genuinely surprised that team members are unfamiliar with or ambivalent about the change vision. Failure to communicate change visions clearly and persistently leads to the sort of cynicism that fuels demands for the products of Despair, a company devoted to ridiculing the motivational posters that too often adorn offices and hallways and are intended to communicate a vision. Despair's (n.d.) riposte to these faux inspirations includes captions such as "Teams: Together, We Can Do the Work of One" and "Meetings: None of Us Is as Dumb as All of Us." The antidote to cynicism is neither threats nor fear but rather authenticity and clarity. While it is not necessary for every team member to agree with the change vision, it is essential for everyone to feel respected. The cynic may undermine the effort, but the skeptics—those who have seen many failed change efforts—deserve a respectful hearing. While the cynics may never be persuaded about the value of a change vision, the skeptics simply want to see the evidence. They have been burned before and will not provide the illusion of buy-in based on blind faith. The good news is that once skeptics have evaluated the evidence and supported the vision, they can be some of the best advocates for change. I have been in these situations, where the skeptic will say to his or her fellow teammates, "I thought Doug was crazy about these grading ideas, and I sat there during his presentation with my arms folded and my defenses up. But the evidence I gathered in my own classroom is clear that these ideas work, and now I'm fully supportive." In order to maximize communication about the change vision, every possible channel must be used, and that includes not only leaders talking about the vision but skeptics making insightful contributions to the discussion.

The fifth mistake Kotter (1995) cites is the failure to remove obstacles to the new vision. These obstacles can include organizational structure, performance-appraisal systems, and cases in which the actions of senior managers are not consistent with the spirit of the change vision. Sometimes these obstacles are structural, such as class schedules that prevent effective collaboration among teachers. Sometimes the obstacles are rooted in policy, adopted decades prior by the governing board and preventing effective leadership change from occurring. Most often, however, the obstacles are tradition and past practice, coupled with a reverence for the past that is elevated over experimentation and innovation for the future.

The sixth mistake is the failure to account for short-term wins (Kotter, 1995). Kotter (1995) has suggested that short-term wins should take place in one to two years, and my research on the subject (Reeves & Eaker, 2019) suggests that exceptional progress can be made in 100-day cycles. Team members cannot wait for annual cycles to maintain daily motivation to engage in the difficult work of change. It is not necessary to wait for long-term results. In the best classes, short-term wins happen every day. Think of the music teacher who, through skillful and immediate feedback, has all students leave class knowing that they are playing their instruments or singing better than they did when class began. Adept teachers have focused learning objectives and quick checks for understanding so that every day is a learning win for students. Similarly, school administrators can do the same with more effective meetings, where critical data points on achievement, attendance, discipline, and so on are celebrated at very frequent intervals.

The seventh mistake is declaring victory too soon (Kotter, 1995). Kotter (1995) suggests that re-engineering efforts are plagued by chaotic change, drastic cost cutting, premature declarations of victory, and, of course, handsome payments to re-engineering consultants. But the aftermath of these celebrations includes the organizational survivors who have to clean up the mess. After a few years, Kotter (1995) explains, there is barely a trace of the change efforts. Similar challenges have plagued quality-improvement efforts, organizational-development plans, and massive training and awareness campaigns. They consume time and resources but are not linked to the essential changes in individual and organizational practices necessary to sustain improved results. While short-term wins are important, they are not enough for long-term success. Even when schools have reduced the failure rate and improved performance, a consistent emphasis on improved teaching and more engaged learning is required to sustain the effort.

The eighth mistake is the failure to link changes to organizational culture (Kotter, 1995). The shift from a change initiative to culture is when new practices are no longer the subject of intensive scrutiny and monitoring but are simply "the way we do things around here." For example, safety initiatives often begin with close monitoring, as lives are at stake. But if safety is to become part of organizational culture, then the norms and routines essential for job safety are simply part of what everyone does. It doesn't take much time to walk down the hallway of a school and see reflections of the culture. When the trash litters the hallway, bulletin boards are out of date, and display cases that might have held exemplary student work are empty, the culture appears to be one of neglect. By contrast, when students and staff warmly greet campus visitors, the hallways gleam, and students and staff immediately pick up the rare bit of trash, the culture is one of pride. "The way we do things around here" is found not in a slogan or on a poster but rather in the thousand acts and omissions that students, faculty, and leaders engage in every day.

HOW TO AVOID AND MINIMIZE MISTAKES

Finding mistakes in change leadership is not a very challenging hunting expedition. The field is full of one failed change after another. Taking decisive steps to avoid and minimize these mistakes is considerably more challenging. We will consider each of the eight mistakes in turn and how to deal with them.

The first mistake, failing to create a sufficient sense of urgency, must start with the change leader looking in the mirror. "Is the change I am leading so urgent that I am ready to stake my career and reputation on it? Am I ready to deal with the resistance, anger, tears, and frayed relationships that may occur in the wake of necessary changes? Do I have the unequivocal support of my board so that when the going gets tough, the board will have my back?" For example, while improved grading policies have great potential to improve student performance, discipline, and school culture, more than one superintendent has told me, "I've seen people get fired over trying to change grading—it's just too heavy of a lift." When fear of resistance is greater than the need to change, then any sense of urgency quickly vanishes. If the organization is not ready for change, the time to withdraw the change effort is before it starts.

The second mistake, understanding a coalition as a legislative body that represents all stakeholders, is associated with the well-intentioned effort to be inclusive. While respectful inclusivity is important, it is essential that decision roles are clear up front. This is a group for learning, deliberation, and recommendation. It is not a legislative body that votes on proposals, and it is not a bargaining unit that negotiates with senior leadership. Most importantly, it is not an assembly of staff whose number-one objective is self-preservation. Technologist and physicist Safi Bahcall (2019) explains that every team has people who are focused either on their own career advancement or on the vision of the organization. When the careerists hold sway, then the risk taking necessary for innovation and meaningful change is impossible. But how can the change leader who hired colleagues, assuring them of their opportunities for career advancement, suddenly say their career interests are no longer relevant? The key is the creation of a safe space for deliberation, contrary views, experimentation, and an unending respect for evidence. This can be accomplished with clear group norms, such as directing comments at an idea rather than at a person. In cases where people are reluctant to engage in vigorous debate and divergent thinking, the leader may need to assign roles so that decision alternatives can be examined carefully from different perspectives. Part of advancing one's career in an organization undergoing change is the replacement of a command, control, and obedience culture with one in which people in any level of the hierarchy can appeal to evidence and challenge ideas of those more senior in rank, and have the response be appreciation rather than resentment. The safest airlines have a culture in which copilots and flight attendants can challenge the pilot. The safest operating suites are those in which a nurse can challenge a surgeon. The safest kitchens are those in which a server can point out an error to the chef. The best schools are those in which educators and administrators can test ideas, debate alternatives, and remain friends at the end of the meeting. They can also challenge prevailing practices that can be improved, without challenging the integrity and professionalism of the educators who have been using those polices. Airliners, hospitals, kitchens, and schools are all notoriously hierarchical institutions, but when authority dominates to the point that mistakes cannot be identified, challenged, and rectified, disaster can follow. Leaders may impulsively want to include only people in their inner circle who get it, who buy in, and who reflexively agree with them. This is the path of ruin. Too many teams, especially at the executive level, are based on the desire of participants to be near the seat of power rather than the need of the organization to maximize the use of every person's time and talent. It is not unusual to see executive teams include two dozen people or more. While this may have the illusion of inclusivity, such excessive participation has the opposite effect. Meeting participants see that the discussion is dominated by a few senior leaders, relegating the rest to the status of an audience rather than genuine partner in the deliberations at hand. In order to avoid these challenges, every team—especially one with responsibility for guiding a change vision—must have a charter that is clear, compelling, and public. It must be clear that the purpose of this team is to learn, deliberate, and make recommendations. It is not the place to make presentations or listen to them—all the learning should happen before each meeting starts. The focus is on deliberation, consideration of alternatives, and making recommendations to senior leadership.

When it comes to the third mistake, having an unclear vision, note that groups of people may execute a vision, but it is very unlikely that a large group can create a vision. The evidence from several sources suggests that when the size of a team exceeds seven, meaningful deliberation and participation declines (Mankins & Garton, 2017; Rogelberg, 2019; Yaeger, 2016). In order to have power to propel deep change, the vision must be focused, crystal clear, and compelling.

Here is one vision statement among the seventy-nine professor Chris Drew (n.d.) has collected:

> Our vision is to forge strong, positive connections with students so they can achieve independence, build confidence, and gain academic knowledge.
>
> We aim to develop well-rounded and thoughtful students prepared to cope with a changing post-modern and globalized world.
>
> We strive to provide our graduates with an academic foundation that will enable them to gain admission to the colleges or universities of their choice as well as to succeed in those institutions.

Compare the preceding statement to that of the Advent School (n.d.) in Boston: "Learn with passion, act with courage, and change the world." That's a vision teachers and students find compelling and clear, and it guides their daily work. A similarly focused vision might be something like, "All our students exemplify integrity, service, and academic excellence and graduate able to succeed at the school or career of their choice." I am not arguing that this should be the vision for your school. But Kotter's (1995) fundamental point remains—when visions are unclear, their persuasive power is diminished.

In the organizations I have led, I have had one consistent cardinal rule, which happens to naturally minimize mistake four, failure to communicate a clear vision: *no one should ever be fired for too much communication*. In survey after survey, employees list more communication as one of their highest needs and greatest recommendations for improvement, yet organizations persist in communicating in much the same way as they have for generations—staff meetings and newsletters. If a change vision is important enough to disrupt the organization, it is important enough to be communicated with the same intensity, frequency, and creativity that would be used for the organization's most important activities. In order to accomplish this, the communication plan should be developed before the vision is articulated, so that when the vision is complete, a multichannel strategy is deployed to get the word out and—here is the piece that most organizations forget—provide multiple checks for understanding to see whether the vision is understood. The least-persuasive communication plan for schools is reliance on a single method, such as email. The most-effective communication plans include multiple methods, including personal calls, home visits, newsletters in languages that parents speak, texts, videos, and every other method appropriate for a specific community. School communities are diverse and complex places, so different methods of communication, including person-to-person communication, are essential. Rather than surveys, organizations can create incentives for team members to participate actively in communication and help to creatively share their insights about the vision with colleagues. If communication about the vision is the exclusive province of the communications department or an outside advertising and communications firm, expect to see more Despair posters on the wall—or at least the same images on coffee cups hidden away on desks. Jeffrey Pfeffer (2015) reminds us that there are more important characteristics than inspiration in vision statements, and foremost among them is authenticity. People will pursue visions that are aspirational, but they will not pursue fantasies and bluster, particularly if they have been through a few rounds of change based on magical thinking in the past. The vision itself and the way in which it is communicated, along with the leadership actions associated with the change, will allow team members to judge the authenticity of the vision and the integrity of the leaders.

Removing obstacles to change, or minimizing the fifth mistake, requires a deep understanding of why the change is needed in the first place. If, for example, an organization is attempting to accelerate the rate of responsiveness to external and internal customers, there may be organizational and hierarchical barriers to speed and responsiveness. If they are seeking to improve safety, there may be internal regulations with multiple supervisory safety inspections that stand in the way of employees taking responsibility for safety. The most pervasive cultural barrier to change is the climate of fear, in which there is the suspicion that people who try new things and take risks will be punished for less-than-perfect results. Leaders who attempt to create organizational change while maintaining a climate of fear cannot blame their subordinates for being resistant to change. The resistance is the result of the climate the leader created. There must be a no-blame zone surrounding important change efforts, especially when the change requires new practices, new tools, and new ideas that are unfamiliar to those expected to implement them. Thus, the biggest obstacles to be removed are not the people who the leader believes are insufficiently supportive of change. Rather, the biggest obstacles are the structures, culture, and climate for which the leader is responsible. In schools, the more common cultural obstacle to change is the presumption of autonomy. Teachers understandably value their ability to be creative in the classroom. Part of their professional identity is a sense of independence, especially with regard to instruction, assessment, discipline, and grading. But another part of being a professional is adhering to a common set of standards that define any profession, including medicine, law, accounting, and others. It is simply not true that professional autonomy is unlimited. Many people, for example, might say that teachers do not have the autonomy to inflict corporal punishment on students. Yet we routinely tolerate what I would call *academic corporal punishment*, with inconsistent discipline policies and demonstrably inaccurate and ineffective grading practices. Just as a few teachers account for a disproportionate number of failures, so, too, do a few teachers typically account for a disproportionate number of discipline referrals. While it is essential to have a safe classroom environment, the best way to achieve that is to have norms in place and to teach students expected behaviors. Every time teachers discipline students for ambiguous offenses, such as *disrespect*, and every time leaders tolerate these practices, they reinforce a culture that will make essential changes nearly impossible. The essential cultural change is from private practice, with arbitrary and individual decisions, to collective responsibility for student success.

Creating short-term wins, or avoiding the sixth mistake, can start with a systematic examination of the practices of the leadership team, coalition, and other groups responsible for the implementation of the change vision. I have seen teams that have tolerated inefficient and toxic behaviors for years change suddenly when they made a commitment to engage in objective self-assessment at the end of every meeting. If they have norms that involve everyone participating, expressing an understanding of alternative points of view, and deliberately considering options before making a recommendation, then a two-minute check at the end of each meeting will yield a scale from zero to four of how consistent that meeting was with group norms. If teams start with small weekly scores like this, they will find other ways to monitor and publicly report their progress, setbacks, and small wins that lead to long-term results. Celebrations of short-term wins require not elaborate festivities but simple and sincere appreciation. It's also useful to ask individuals and teams how they prefer to be recognized. Some people appreciate public recognition while others would prefer a personal note or private expression of thanks for their successful efforts. The key to small wins is that they are part of a cycle of reinforcing individual and team efforts that go into successful change.

As important as small wins are, they are only mileposts on the marathon of change, so it's critical not to declare victory too soon—the seventh mistake. While the marathon analogy is overused, my seven marathons, including Boston's, allow me to make the analogy about more than distance. In the Marine Corps Marathon in and around Washington, DC, the 26.2-mile course is the same length as every other marathon around the world; however, there is a key difference. It's not unusual that the last half mile of a marathon is designed to be easy. For the Twin Cities Marathon, for example, runners complete the course passing the cathedral in St. Paul following a gentle downhill slope. San Francisco offers a similar glide that has the last half of the race proceeding from the Golden Gate Bridge to the Embarcadero. Boston, famous for Heartbreak Hill, has the finish line on flat Commonwealth Avenue. Not so for the Marine Corps Marathon. The last half mile, when most participants are exhausted, takes you uphill, toward the Iwo Jima Memorial, the iconic statue of six soldiers hoisting the flag. Despite the uphill climb, everyone finishes as this inspiring vision draws every runner to an emotionally charged conclusion. The victory is not, in brief, downhill, and nobody thinks that the race is over at the twentieth mile. Change leaders must therefore maintain the momentum not just during the planning of the change process but throughout the change until they cross the finish line.

Avoiding the eighth mistake, or successfully linking changes to organizational culture, begins with the idea that culture is simply the congruence between behavior and belief. When a school glorifies rhetoric about equity but maintains policies that undermine student access to gifted and talented programs or Advanced Placement classes, then the tolerance of inequity outweighs the rhetoric of equity. When the rhetoric is in favor of standards and against the bell curve, but evaluation practices continue to compare students to one another rather than to a standard, then the rhetoric of standards is impotent. When posters on the wall carry the rhetoric of teaching excellence, but administrators give positive evaluations to mediocre and inadequate teaching, then the culture of mediocrity overwhelms the rhetoric of excellence.

CONCLUSION

Change leadership is fraught with risk, so it must be undertaken only when the leader is virtually certain that the pain of change is worth the gain. One way to reduce the pain is to anticipate the mistakes inherent in the change process and take deliberate actions to mitigate those risks. Of all the common mistakes in this chapter, the failure to communicate a sense of urgency is the most important. When students fail, and especially when those failures prevent them from gaining high school diplomas, there is a lifetime of consequences not only for those students but also for their communities. Thus, the sense of urgency we must communicate on the deep changes required for student success is not just about a single student; it's about the lifetime of negative consequences if schools and districts fail to implement change.

REFLECTION

Review the following prompts, and record your responses someplace where you can easily refer to them throughout the deep change journey.

1. Consider a change initiative you have seen, either in education or in other parts of your life, that floundered. As you think about the principal causes of mistakes in change efforts, which ones were relevant to the change initiative you've identified?
2. What change do you need right now, either professionally or personally? Describe why this change is urgent, and, if you are working with a team to implement the change, describe how you will create a sense of urgency for team members.

Chapter 12

Building a Team for Deep Change

If you are a change leader, do you have a team or an audience? Here's one way to find out. Go to a meeting, exchange greetings with your team members, and explain to your colleagues that today you'd just like to listen. And then say absolutely nothing. In a high-performing team, members will without hesitation begin the discussion, follow team norms, and encourage and challenge one another in equal measure. However, if, in the absence of leadership direction, the team is paralyzed, then you know that you don't really have a team; you have an audience. As Roger M. Schwarz (2013) notes in *Smart Leaders, Smarter Teams,* when there is only one leader in the room, the probability of that team getting and staying stuck is very high. The fundamental reason that teams get stuck is a lack of trust and the consequent unwillingness to take risks and test alternative ideas and solutions in the cauldron of respectful but intense debate. This chapter considers the power of networks and what makes for a great team of change leaders.

THE POWER OF NETWORKS

In the magnificent book *Linked: How Everything Is Connected to Everything Else and What It Means for Business, Science, and Everyday Life* by Albert-László Barabási

(2014), a network scientist at Northeastern University, the subtitle says it all: everything is connected to everything else. This is not the parlor trick adapted from the play *Six Degrees of Separation,* in which the conceit is that we are all connected in our human relationships to one another. Rather, Barabási's compelling research shows there are profoundly influential network hubs, both human and inanimate, that have a disproportionate influence on an ever-expanding network. These network hubs can include people of exceptional ability, such as Hungarian mathematician Paul Erdős, whose connections throughout the world of mathematics are linked to so many scholars that they have coined the term *Erdős number* to denote the degree of separation from this frantic collaborator. An Erdős number of 1 signifies that the author cowrote with Erdős. The number 2 applies to those who wrote with one of those coauthors, and so on. An astonishing amount of mathematical scholarship of the 20th century is associated with people who had Erdős numbers of 3 or fewer. To make his profound impact, Erdős flew around the world, staying with friends, collaborating for a few days, and moving on (Barabási, 2014).

That laborious mode of collaboration seems primitive in the third decade of the 21st century, when a teenager with a handheld device and a social-media account can reach more people than Erdős dreamed of. Anyone with an opinion and short attention span can share insight on Twitter, and with the flick of a finger, others can retweet that original opinion. The network can be used to instantly share with millions of people everything from health warnings to the location of a fight, from video reviews to unflattering candid photos of celebrities. The networks in the cloud are neither meritocratic nor demonic. They are, like the literal clouds after which they are named, pervasive, fast moving, and impossible to hold. While students were confined to their homes during the spring of 2020, some suffered learning losses due to inadequate access to technology and connectivity. Other students, however, not only thrived but developed networks of students from their neighborhoods and around the globe. The power of networks remain in schools and in life.

Great teams use the power of networks to create team repositories of information, communicate quickly, and, most importantly, immediately check and challenge disinformation. The sheer amount of information coming from networks can be overwhelming, but great teams do not drink information as if from a fire hose. Rather, they collaborate to filter and refine information coming in and also carefully focus the information they transmit so that, like Paul Erdős or the most popular thirteen-year-old fashionista in your neighborhood, people select their communication from the trillions of other bytes of information coming their way.

They do this through brevity—respecting the time of the recipient—and importance. When you receive something from a great team member, you know it is worth reading. Thus, a team of seven can influence and inform an audience of thousands or many more.

WHAT MAKES FOR A GREAT TEAM?

In previous chapters, this book has presented evidence from a wide variety of schools and educational organizations, as well as evidence from business, medicine, and nonprofit organizations. The evidence on effective change and the teams that lead change come from around the globe, representing cultures that range from hierarchical to egalitarian. Despite these differences, however, certain characteristics are consistently associated with great teams. These factors include trust, learning, focus, mutual responsibility, and greater purpose.

TRUST

Great teams are composed of people who trust one another and who trust the team as a whole. Trust is key to a psychologically safe environment, and teams in a high-trust environment learn more, achieve more, and exhibit greater satisfaction than teams with similarly bright people who operate in low-trust environments (Edmondson, 2019). The first time that teachers share their lessons, assessments, and student results with their colleagues, they are depending on their colleagues to view this public act of self-revelation with respect. They know that they can ask questions without seeming impertinent or accusatory and that they can learn from one another. But in a low-trust environment, teachers are unlikely to share their work and even less likely to share their students' work. It takes enormous professional confidence and great trust to engage in meaningful collaboration.

Trust is evident when people can acknowledge mistakes, reconsider previous opinions, and, most importantly, challenge prevailing practices. It is important to carefully define terms here. *Trust* does not mean "Trust me—I know what I'm doing, so I don't need to explain my decisions." *Trust* in the context of great teams means "Of course I trust you, but I need you to trust me enough to allow me to ask questions, challenge assumptions, and learn as much as I can about the conclusion you are proposing." Hospital emergency rooms are high-trust environments, in which many skilled professionals work simultaneously to save lives. Nevertheless, according to public health researcher Atul Gawande (2010), those with the lowest death rates use checklists and have a culture in which any member of the treatment team can challenge the most senior member. It is important that teams distinguish between a learning failure—the sort of error that leads to greater learning and fewer mistakes in the future—and careless failures. Designing a new technique, invention, or drug that does not work is a learning failure. The scientist's maxim is that we learn more from error than from uncertainty. However, failing to wear a mask while stitching up a patient, failing to review a regulatory form, and failing to conduct financial audits, all while other teammates know about and tolerate these failures, are sloppy, intolerable mistakes. Similarly, while most schools claim to value civility and civil discourse, the leader who tolerates intimidation and insults in a faculty meeting undermines those values. Moreover, the norms of civility cannot depend on the leader alone. Norms have the greatest power when everyone on the team is attentive to norms and is courageous enough to call out norm violations.

LEARNING

Great teams engage in systematic learning. Unfortunately, the model of learning that most organizations have is little changed from the one-room schoolhouse on the prairie or the medieval university. What they have in common is that learning, if we can call it that, consists of one teacher distributing information while everyone else attentively listens and copies what they have learned. That is not learning; that is delivery. DuFour and colleagues (2016) demonstrate that it is collaboration around real student work and a discussion of related professional practices that lead to professional learning. Yet many school district cabinet meetings are consumed by slideshows, lectures, and pointless pontificating, all under the guise of group learning. Real learning is interactive, and great teams have an ironclad norm that passive learning—reading or listening—happens before the meetings. During the meetings, great teams deliberate, debate, and consider alternative ways of understanding information. They learn not from presentations but from the contention of ideas and evidence. Often, teams have a member who has particular expertise, such as technology, finance, or law. While such expertise is valuable, team learning does not happen if the experts only deliver information and fail to gain better understanding of how everyone else applies, understands, and misunderstands their expertise. The veteran teacher with little technology experience can be a very valuable member of a team devoted to instructional technology. By asking persistent questions about the value and use of technology interventions, the technologically inexperienced teacher will help the implementation be more effective for the entire school. Moreover, if the learning consists of briefings, with different departments providing status reports to the principal or superintendent, then one person is learning and everyone else is a passive observer. Team learning means that, at the end of every meeting, every team member can say with integrity, "Here is something new I learned today."

FOCUS

In the study of improvement plans I mentioned in chapter 7 (page 75), I found that six or fewer priorities were associated with dramatically better results. While some plans had more than seventy goals and priorities, the most successful plans had no more than a half dozen. Focus is especially difficult in times of success, when organizational resources allow leaders to pursue every available shiny object for organizational development. Focus can also be challenging for organizations in crisis, when leaders are frantically grasping at every imaginable solution. One task I ask leadership teams to engage in is the *not-to-do list,* in which they identify both individual and team practices they will discontinue. For most of them, this is excruciating work, and many complain that it is impossible. Here is the central argument for focus: barring the apocalypse, the end of the current year will arrive, and there will be things that neither you nor your team will finish. Therefore, you already have a not-to-do list—it is just an unconscious list, the things that fell off the table for lack of time and focus. The choice is not whether to have such a list but whether it will be a consciously and deliberately selected list or an unconscious list. Great teams make the wise choice and focus.

MUTUAL RESPONSIBILITY

Great teams share mutual responsibility for both successes and failures. One of the great myths in fields ranging from organizational leadership to creative pursuits is that there is the lonely person at the top who, courageously fighting alone, thinks great thoughts, does great deeds, and saves the day. But the evidence is overwhelmingly to the contrary. Successes in Olympic sports (Harford, 2016), scientific discoveries (Barabási, 2018), creativity (Reeves & Reeves, 2017), and organizational leadership (Edmondson, 2019) are the result of teamwork, not the mythical lone individual. The illusion of the solitary genius is sometimes drawn from the public recognition provided to the winner of the Nobel Prize, Academy Award, or sports championship, or to the CEO of the most admired company. But none of those honors were earned by a single individual. Wise leaders know that even though recognition and praise is disproportionately awarded to a few, and typically to those with the greatest visibility and rank, the recognized success will be short-lived if credit and accompanying rewards are not shared. For team members, sharing credit is a habit, not an act. University of Pennsylvania organizational psychologist Adam Grant (2019b) suggests that one of the most powerful screens in an interview is the number of times a prospective employee refers to "we" rather than "I" when asked about accomplishments. He further suggests that a powerful question is to ask the candidate to name four people the candidate has helped to progress in their careers. The self-oriented candidates will, if they can name anyone, identify people who were above them in the hierarchy—how they helped the boss get his or her next promotion. The team-oriented candidates will, by contrast, talk about how they helped subordinates and peers advance their careers. If a great team member expresses "I," it will be to take personal responsibility for mistakes. While throwing a teammate under the bus for a mistake may be part of the culture of sharp-elbowed, competitive organizations, that behavior should exclude someone from eligibility for membership in a leadership team.

GREATER PURPOSE

Great teams have a greater purpose (Yaeger, 2016). When the challenges are exceptional and team members need the energy to break through the fog of fatigue and adversity, then only a common purpose will ignite the energy necessary to sustain the work. I've seen teams keep photos of students and families displayed prominently in meetings so that they are always aware of their greater service—helping students learn, grow, and serve. Every employee is a volunteer, and while pay and benefits are important, they are not sufficient to motivate employees. That is particularly true of people who are members of or aspire to join leadership teams.

CONCLUSION

In this chapter, we considered the characteristics of a great team: trust, learning, focus, mutual responsibility, and greater purpose. Teams deploy the power of networks not with immense quantities of transmissions but with judicious and brief transmissions of information so vital that recipients elevate the communications from the team above all the clutter of the network. They also collaborate to filter incoming information and provide a reality check for the disinformation that is pervasive—especially about organizational-change efforts. Finally, teams of change leaders take the risk to reject 20th century change models and accelerate the pace and magnify the impact of change.

REFLECTION

Review the following prompts, and record your responses someplace where you can easily refer to them throughout the deep change journey.

1. Think of a team you have been a part of, either in education or in the larger community, that was remarkably effective. Trust was high, and team members were active learners. Members shared a greater purpose that propelled their commitment and work. As you think about that team of change leaders, how can you replicate its success in your school?
2. Consider a team on which you are now serving—anything from a grade-level team to a district cabinet. What is one thing the team could do immediately to improve trust and learning?

Epilogue

Iceberg Ahead

The climactic scene in the movie *Titanic* begins with the sailor on the bridge looking into the night sky, full of fog and the sound of waves. Then, in a matter of seconds, a terrifying object fills the screen. "Iceberg—right ahead!" the sailor screams (Cameron, 1997). But whether or not you saw the movie, you know the end of the story. It was too late to avoid disaster.

The differences between that *Titanic* and educational icebergs that we face in the 21st century are as follows: The speed of the ship is much faster, in that the schools we serve experience dramatic changes in demographics, technology, and student needs. The size of the icebergs—and there are many of them—is enormous, with challenges including poverty, the aftermath of the pandemic and associated learning losses, and financial stresses on school systems. However insufficient the lifeboats on the *Titanic* may have been, there are even fewer lifeboats for schools in treacherous waters today. Those who have written the obituary of public education might suggest that we just abandon ship. But we don't need lifeboats—we need to keep our students safe and keep the ship afloat.

The image of an oceangoing vessel, especially in the context of the *Titanic*, suggests not only potential failure but also a pace of change that is slow. But the need for change—deep change—is immediate. Students and schools can fail with astonishing rapidity. Educational systems heralded for best practices one year are just a few years later caught in a merry-go-round of leadership changes and the chaos that accompanies it. So is it just hopeless? The lessons of this book are that while the need for change remains significant and pervasive, change leaders can dramatically reduce risk if they develop the ability to effect deep change that combines quick wins with long-term sustainable improvements in leadership, teaching, and student performance.

Those who find change overwhelmingly challenging will often use the metaphor that organizational change is like turning around an aircraft carrier. This is the perfect analogy, because the claim presumes that the behemoth vessel carrying five thousand sailors, aviators, and marines; hauling aircraft and equipment; and weighing more than fifty metric tons must be nearly impossible to turn. After hearing this belabored illustration used a few too many times, I called my brother, Steve, who at the time was a two-star general with a global command that included soldiers, sailors, aviators, and marines. I asked him how long it really took to turn around an aircraft carrier. He called the deck of the USS *Nimitz* and inquired. The answer? Depending on sea conditions, between three and eleven minutes. So much for another tired military analogy. Even in large complex organizations in challenging environments, we can make change—we can turn the aircraft carrier around with much more agility than people think.

Let us return to the bridge of the *Titanic*. The iceberg wouldn't move. The design of the ship could have been better, but it was too late to change the ship's design. The only thing the captain could have done was to turn—and turn quickly. The *Titanic* didn't have that sort of turning capacity, and perhaps the crew of a passenger liner was unprepared to make such an abrupt maneuver in any case lest it cause discomfort among the passengers. But you can. With the tools you've learned in these pages, you can turn your schools and districts in the right direction. I've seen it done in large urban schools and small rural schools, in schools that had experienced years of chronic low academic performance and in high-performing schools that made decisive deep changes to get even better. Deep change can happen. The only question is whether we are willing to lead it.

References and Resources

Adams, M. (2015). *Change your questions, change your life: 12 powerful tools for leadership, coaching, and life* (3rd ed.). Oakland, CA: Berrett-Koehler.

Advent School. (n.d.). *Learn, act, change: Advent's strategic plan*. Accessed at https://adventschool.org/welcome/strategic-plan/ on November 20, 2020.

Amabile, T., & Kramer, S. (2011). *The progress principle: Using small wins to ignite joy, engagement, and creativity at work*. Boston: Harvard Business Review Press.

Anderson, R. J., & Adams, W. A. (2019). *Scaling leadership: Building organizational capability and capacity to create outcomes that matter most*. Hoboken, NJ: Wiley.

Anthony, S. D., Trotter, A., & Schwartz, E. I. (2019, September 24). The top 20 business transformations of the last decade. *Harvard Business Review*. Accessed at https://hbr.org/2019/09/the-top-20-business-transformations-of-the-last-decade on July 21, 2020.

Ates, N. Y., Tarakci, M., Porck, J. P., van Knippenberg, D., & Groenen, P. (2019, February 28). Why visionary leadership fails. *Harvard Business Review*. Accessed at https://hbr.org/2019/02/why-visionary-leadership-fails on July 21, 2020.

Bahcall, S. (2019). *Loonshots: How to nurture the crazy ideas that win wars, cure diseases, and transform industries*. New York: St. Martin's Press.

Barabási, A.-L. (2014). *Linked: How everything is connected to everything else and what it means for business, science, and everyday life*. New York: Basic Books.

Barabási, A.-L. (2018). *The formula: The universal laws of success.* New York: Little, Brown.

Baumeister, R. F., & Tierney, J. (2011). *Willpower: Rediscovering the greatest human strength.* New York: Penguin.

Beer, M., Finnström, M., & Schrader, D. (2016, October). Why leadership training fails—and what to do about it. *Harvard Business Review.* Accessed at https://hbr.org/2016/10/why-leadership-training-fails-and-what-to-do-about-it on July 21, 2020.

Blank, S. (2019, October 7). Why companies do "innovation theater" instead of actual innovation. *Harvard Business Review.* Accessed at https://hbr.org/2019/10/why-companies-do-innovation-theater-instead-of-actual-innovation?ab=hero-subleft-3 on July 21, 2020.

Borg-Laufs, M. (2013). Basic psychological needs in childhood and adolescence. *Journal of Education and Research, 3*(1), 41–51.

Botelho, E. L., Powell, K. R., Kincaid, S., & Wang, D. (2017, May–June). What sets successful CEOs apart. *Harvard Business Review.* Accessed at https://hbr.org/2017/05/what-sets-successful-ceos-apart on July 21, 2020.

Boyatzis, R. E., Smith, M., & Van Oosten, E. (2019). *Helping people change: Coaching with compassion for lifelong learning and growth.* Boston: Harvard Business Review Press.

Brafman, O., & Brafman, R. (2008). *Sway: The irresistible pull of irrational behavior.* New York: Doubleday.

Bregman, P. (2011). *18 minutes: Find your focus, master distraction, and get the right things done.* New York: Business Plus.

Bregman, P. (2015a). *Four seconds: All the time you need to stop counter-productive habits and get the results you want.* New York: HarperOne.

Bregman, P. (2015b, November 2). 3 timeless rules for making tough decisions. *Harvard Business Review.* Accessed at https://hbr.org/2015/11/3-timeless-rules-for-making-tough-decisions on July 21, 2020.

Brewer, J. (2017). *The craving mind: From cigarettes to smartphones to love—Why we get hooked and how we can break bad habits.* New Haven, CT: Yale University Press.

Brown, T. (2019). *Change by design: How design thinking transforms organizations and inspires innovation* (Revised and updated ed.). New York: HarperBusiness.

Brubaker, M., & Mitchell, C. (2018, July 9). 4 signs an executive isn't ready for coaching. *Harvard Business Review.* Accessed at https://hbr.org/2018/07/4-signs-an-executive-isnt-ready-for-coaching on July 21, 2020.

Buckingham, M., & Goodall, A. (2019). *Nine lies about work: A freethinking leader's guide to the real world.* Boston: Harvard Business Review Press.

Burns, W. J. (2019). *The back channel: A memoir of American diplomacy and the case for its renewal.* New York: Random House.

Cameron, J. (Producer & Director). (1997). *Titanic* [Motion picture]. United States: Paramount Pictures.

Carucci, R. (2016a, January 19). A 10-year study reveals what great executives know and do. *Harvard Business Review*. Accessed at https://hbr.org/2016/01/a-10-year-study-reveals-what-great-executives-know-and-do on July 21, 2020.

Carucci, R. (2016b, October 24). Organizations can't change if leaders can't change with them. *Harvard Business Review*. Accessed at https://hbr.org/2016/10/organizations-cant-change-if-leaders-cant-change-with-them on July 21, 2020.

Carucci, R. (2018a, July 16). What not to do when you're trying to motivate your team. *Harvard Business Review*. Accessed at https://hbr.org/2018/07/what-not-to-do-when-youre-trying-to-motivate-your-team on July 21, 2020.

Carucci, R. (2018b, December 13). When a leader is causing conflict, start by asking why. *Harvard Business Review*. Accessed at https://hbr.org/2018/12/when-a-leader-is-causing-conflict-start-by-asking-why on July 21, 2020.

Carucci, R. (2019, August 6). Leading change in a company that's historically bad at it. *Harvard Business Review*. Accessed at https://hbr.org/2019/08/leading-change-in-a-company-thats-historically-bad-at-it on July 21, 2020.

Centola, D. (2018). *How behavior spreads: The science of complex contagions*. Princeton, NJ: Princeton University Press.

Chavez, T., O'Hara, C., & Vaidya, V. (2019). *Data driven: Harnessing data and AI to reinvent customer engagement*. New York: McGraw-Hill Education.

Chesanow, N. (2014). *Why are so many patients noncompliant?* Accessed at www.medscape.com/viewarticle/818850 on July 21, 2020.

Christensen, C. M., Hall, T., Dillon, K., & Duncan, D. S. (2016). *Competing against luck: The story of innovation and customer choice*. New York: HarperBusiness.

Christensen, C. M., Horn, M. B., & Johnson, C. W. (2011). *Disrupting class: How disruptive innovation will change the way the world learns* (Updated and expanded new ed.). New York: McGraw-Hill.

Clear, J. (2018). *Atomic habits: Tiny changes, remarkable results—An easy and proven way to build good habits and break bad ones*. New York: Avery.

Cloud, H. (2018). *Changes that heal: Four practical steps to a happier, healthier you*. Grand Rapids, MI: Zondervan.

Colonna, J. (2019). *Reboot: Leadership and the art of growing up*. New York: HarperBusiness.

Connors, R., & Smith, T. (2011). *Change the culture, change the game: The breakthrough strategy for energizing your organization and creating accountability for results*. New York: Portfolio Penguin.

Constable, J. (2018, March 28). Two techniques for helping employees change ingrained habits. *Harvard Business Review*. Accessed at https://hbr.org/2018/03/two-techniques-for-helping-employees-change-ingrained-habits on July 21, 2020.

Covey, S. M. R. (2006). *The speed of trust: The one thing that changes everything*. New York: Free Press.

Coyle, D. (2018). *The culture code: The secrets of highly successful groups*. New York: Bantam Books.

Cran, C. (2015). *The art of change leadership: Driving transformation in a fast-paced world*. Hoboken, NJ: Wiley.

Crenshaw, D. (2008). *The myth of multitasking: How "doing it all" gets nothing done*. San Francisco: Jossey-Bass.

Crutchfield, L. R. (2018). *How change happens: Why some social movements succeed while others don't*. Hoboken, NJ: Wiley.

Csikszentmihalyi, M. (1990). *Flow: The psychology of optimal experience*. New York: Harper & Row.

Danielson, C. (2013). *The framework for teaching evaluation instrument*. Princeton, NJ: Danielson Group.

Danielson, C., & McGreal, T. L. (2000). *Teacher evaluation to enhance professional practice*. Alexandria, VA: Association for Supervision and Curriculum Development.

de Montaigne, M. (1993). *The complete essays* (M. A. Screech, Trans.). London: Penguin.

Despair. (n.d.). *Demotivational posters*. Accessed at https://despair.com/collections/posters on November 20, 2020.

DeSteno, D. (2018). *Emotional success: The power of gratitude, compassion, and pride*. Boston: Houghton Mifflin Harcourt.

Deutschman, A. (2007). *Change or die: The three keys to change at work and in life*. New York: Regan.

Dobbs, R. (2010). *Transformational leadership: A blueprint for real organizational change*. Little Rock, AR: Parkhurst.

Dodgson, L. (2018, December 31). *The psychology behind why we're so bad at keeping New Year's resolutions*. Accessed at www.insider.com/the-psychology-behind-why-we-cant-keep-new-years-resolutions-2018-1 on September 13, 2020.

Doerr, J. (2018). *Measure what matters: How Google, Bono, and the Gates Foundation rock the world with OKRs*. New York: Penguin.

Drake, G. (2018, April 19). *Reading into flat NAEP scores* [Blog post]. Accessed at www.nctq.org/blog/Reading-into-flat-NAEP-scores on October 18, 2020.

Drew, C. (n.d.). *79 examples of school vision and mission statements*. Accessed at https://helpfulprofessor.com/school-vision-and-mission-statements/ on November 20, 2020.

Duckworth, A. (2016). *Grit: The power of passion and perseverance.* New York: Scribner.

Duffy, S. (2018). *Breakthrough: How to harness the aha! moments that spark success.* Irvine, CA: Entrepreneur Press.

DuFour, R., DuFour, R., Eaker, R., Many, T. W., & Mattos, M. (2016). *Learning by doing: A handbook for Professional Learning Communities at Work* (3rd ed.). Bloomington, IN: Solution Tree Press.

DuFour, R., & Reeves, D. (2016). The futility of PLC Lite. *Phi Delta Kappan, 97*(6), 69–71.

DuFour, R., Reeves, D., & DuFour, R. (2018). *Responding to the Every Student Succeeds Act with the PLC at Work process.* Bloomington, IN: Solution Tree Press.

Duke, A. (2018). *Thinking in bets: Making smarter decisions when you don't have all the facts.* New York: Portfolio/Penguin.

Dutton, J. E., & Spreitzer, G. M. (Eds.). (2014). *How to be a positive leader: Small actions, big impact.* San Francisco: Berrett-Koehler.

Dyson, J. (2011, April 8). No innovator's dilemma here: In praise of failure. *Wired.* Accessed at www.wired.com/2011/04/in-praise-of-failure/ on August 17, 2020.

Eberhardt, J. L. (2019). *Biased: Uncovering the hidden prejudice that shapes what we see, think, and do.* New York: Viking.

Edmondson, A. C. (2012). *Teaming: How organizations learn, innovate, and compete in the knowledge economy.* San Francisco: Jossey-Bass.

Edmondson, A. C. (2019). *The fearless organization: Creating psychological safety in the workplace for learning, innovation, and growth.* Hoboken, NJ: Wiley.

Ellen MacArthur Foundation & IDEO. (n.d.). *The circular design guide.* Accessed at www.circulardesignguide.com/ on July 21, 2020.

Emerson, R. W. (2017). *Self-reliance and other essays.* Seattle, WA: AmazonClassics.

Epstein, D. (2019). *Range: Why generalists triumph in a specialized world.* New York: Riverhead Books.

Ericsson, A., & Pool, R. (2016). *Peak: Secrets from the new science of expertise.* Boston: Houghton Mifflin Harcourt.

Eurich, T. (2018). *Insight: The surprising truth about how others see us, how we see ourselves, and why the answers matter more than we think.* New York: Currency.

Every Student Succeeds Act of 2015, Pub. L. No. 114-95, 20 U.S.C. § 1177 (2015).

Eyal, N. (2019). *Indistractable: How to control your attention and choose your life.* Dallas, TX: BenBella Books.

Firestein, S. (2012). *Ignorance: How it drives science.* New York: Oxford University Press.

Flounder. (n.d.). In *Cambridge Dictionary.* Accessed at https://dictionary.cambridge.org/us/dictionary/english/flounder?q=floundering on July 21, 2020.

Fullan, M. (2008). *The six secrets of change: What the best leaders do to help their organizations survive and thrive.* San Francisco: Jossey-Bass.

Fullan, M. (2011). *Change leader: Learning to do what matters most.* San Francisco: Jossey-Bass.

Fullan, M. (2019). *Nuance: Why some leaders succeed and others fail.* Thousand Oaks, CA: Corwin Press.

Fundbox Team. (2020). *Why profitable businesses fail, and how to fix it.* Accessed at www.fundera.com/blog/why-profitable-businesses-fail-and-how-to-fix-it on July 21, 2020.

Galbraith, M. (2018, October 5). Don't just tell employees organizational changes are coming—explain why. *Harvard Business Review.* Accessed at https://hbr.org/2018/10/dont-just-tell-employees-organizational-changes-are-coming-explain-why on July 21, 2020.

Gardner, H. (1999). *Intelligence reframed: Multiple intelligences for the 21st century.* New York: Basic Books.

Gardner, H. (Ed.). (2007). *Responsibility at work: How leading professionals act (or don't act) responsibly.* San Francisco: Jossey-Bass.

Gardner, H. (2011). *Frames of mind: The theory of multiple intelligences.* New York: Basic Books.

Garrett, R., & Steinberg, M. P. (2015). Examining teacher effectiveness using classroom observation scores: Evidence from the randomization of teachers to students. *Educational Evaluation and Policy Analysis, 37*(2), 224–242.

Gary, L. (2002). Fostering change while avoiding the road to martyrdom. *Harvard Management Update, 7*(4), 7–8.

Gawande, A. (2010). *The checklist manifesto: How to get things right.* New York: Metropolitan Books.

Gino, F. (2018, August 22). Case study: Can you fix a toxic culture without firing people? *Harvard Business Review.* Accessed at https://hbr.org/2018/08/case-study-can-you-fix-a-toxic-culture-without-firing-people on July 21, 2020.

Gladwell, M. (2008). *Outliers: The story of success.* New York: Little, Brown.

Gladwell, M. (2019). *Talking to strangers: What we should know about the people we don't know.* New York: Little, Brown.

Goleman, D. (2013). *Focus: The hidden driver of excellence.* New York: Harper.

Goleman, D., Boyatzis, R., & McKee, A. (2002). *Primal leadership: Realizing the power of emotional intelligence.* Boston: Harvard Business School Press.

Goleman, D., & Nevarez, M. (2018, August 16). Boost your emotional intelligence with these 3 questions. *Harvard Business Review.* Accessed at https://hbr.org/2018/08/boost-your-emotional-intelligence-with-these-3-questions on July 21, 2020.

Goodstein, L. (2008, July 11). Serenity prayer stirs up doubt: Who wrote it? *The New York Times*. Accessed at www.nytimes.com/2008/07/11/us/11prayer.html on July 21, 2020.

Goodwin, D. K. (2005). *Team of rivals: The political genius of Abraham Lincoln*. New York: Simon & Schuster.

Goodwin, D. K. (2018). *Leadership in turbulent times*. New York: Simon & Schuster.

Gopnik, A., Meltzoff, A. N., & Kuhl, P. K. (1999). *The scientist in the crib: Minds, brains, and how children learn*. New York: Morrow.

Gould, S. J. (1981). *The mismeasure of man*. New York: Norton.

Gould, S. J. (2008). *The mismeasure of man* (Rev. and expanded ed.). New York: Norton.

Gouré, D. (2018). *Winning future wars: Modernization and a 21st century defense industrial base*. Accessed at www.heritage.org/military-strength-topical-essays/2019-essays/winning-future-wars-modernization-and-21st-century on July 21, 2020.

Grant, A. (2016). *Originals: How non-conformists move the world*. New York: Viking.

Grant, A. (2019a). *Power moves: Lessons from Davos* [Audiobook]. Newark, NJ: Audible Originals.

Grant, A. (2019b, February 5). The surprising value of obvious insights. *MIT Sloan Management Review*. Accessed at https://sloanreview.mit.edu/article/the-surprising-value-of-obvious-insights/ on July 21, 2020.

Green, D. (2016). *How change happens*. Oxford, England: Oxford University Press.

Greenberg, R. (n.d.). *The symphonies of Beethoven*. Accessed at https://robertgreenbergmusic.com/download/beethoven-symphonies/ on November 16, 2020.

Gregoire, C. (2013). *Why 'follow your passion' is bad career advice*. Accessed at www.huffpost.com/entry/sustainable-career_n_3618480?guccounter=1 on July 21, 2020.

Grenny, J., Patterson, K., Maxfield, D., McMillan, R., & Switzler, A. (2013). *Influencer: The new science of leading change* (2nd ed.). New York: McGraw-Hill Education.

Grivas, C., & Puccio, G. J. (2012). *The innovative team: Unleashing creative potential for breakthrough results*. San Francisco: Jossey-Bass.

Guinness, H. (2019, December 2). You should start practicing New Year's resolutions now. *The New York Times*. Accessed at www.nytimes.com/2019/12/02/smarter-living/new-years-resolutions.html?searchResultPosition=1 on July 21, 2020.

Guskey, T. R. (2020a). *Get set, go: Creating successful grading and reporting systems*. Bloomington, IN: Solution Tree Press.

Guskey, T. R. (2020b). Flip the script on change. *The Learning Professional, 41*(2), 18–22.

Haden, J. (2018). *The motivation myth: How high achievers really set themselves up to win*. New York: Portfolio/Penguin.

Hall, E. (2020). *Aristotle's way: How ancient wisdom can change your life*. New York: Penguin Books.

Hamel, G. (2002). *Leading the revolution: How to thrive in turbulent times by making innovation a way of life*. New York: Plume.

Hammer, M., & Champy, J. (1993). *Reengineering the corporation: A manifesto for business revolution*. New York: HarperBusiness.

Hansen, M. T. (2018). *Great at work: The hidden habits of top performers*. New York: Simon & Schuster.

Harari, Y. N. (2015). *Sapiens: A brief history of humankind*. New York: Harper.

Harford, T. (2011). *Adapt: Why success always starts with failure*. New York: Farrar, Straus and Giroux.

Harford, T. (2016). *Messy: The power of disorder to transform our lives*. New York: Riverhead Books.

Hargrave, J. (2016). *Mind hacking: How to change your mind for good in 21 days*. New York: Gallery Books.

Hattie, J. (2009). *Visible learning: A synthesis of over 800 meta-analyses relating to achievement*. London: Routledge.

Hattie, J. (2012). *Visible learning for teachers: Maximizing impact on learning*. London: Routledge.

Hayward, S. (2018). *The agile leader: How to create an agile business in the digital age*. New York: Kogan Page.

Heath, C., & Heath, D. (2010). *Switch: How to change things when change is hard*. New York: Broadway Books.

Heath, C., & Heath, D. (2013). *Decisive: How to make better choices in life and work*. New York: Crown Business.

Herrnstein, R. J., & Murray, C. (1994). *The bell curve: Intelligence and class structure in American life*. New York: Free Press.

Hess, F. (2018, June 12). *Education reforms should obey Campbell's Law* [Blog post]. Accessed at www.educationnext.org/education-reforms-obey-campbells-law/ on July 21, 2020.

Hougaard, R., & Carter, J. (2018, November 6). Ego is the enemy of good leadership. *Harvard Business Review*. Accessed at https://hbr.org/2018/11/ego-is-the-enemy-of-good-leadership on July 21, 2020.

Hutchinson, A. (2018). *Endure: Mind, body, and the curiously elastic limits of human performance*. New York: Morrow.

IBM. (n.d.). *The PC: Personal computing comes of age—in their words*. Accessed at www.ibm.com/ibm/history/ibm100/us/en/icons/personalcomputer/words/ on August 18, 2020.

Ignatius, A. (2015, April). Time to kill forced rankings? *Harvard Business Review*. Accessed at https://hbr.org/2015/04/time-to-kill-forced-rankings on July 21, 2020.

Insurance Institute for Highway Safety. (2020, February). *Distracted driving*. Accessed at www.iihs.org/topics/distracted-driving on August 12, 2020.

Irvine, W. B. (2019). *The stoic challenge: A philosopher's guide to becoming tougher, calmer, and more resilient*. New York: Norton.

Jacobs, A. (2017). *How to think: A survival guide for a world at odds*. New York: Currency.

Johansen, B. (2017). *The new leadership literacies: Thriving in a future of extreme disruption and distributed everything*. Oakland, CA: Berrett-Koehler.

Johnson, A. (2016). *The little book of big change: The no-willpower approach to breaking any habit*. Oakland, CA: New Harbinger Publications.

Johnson, S. (2018a). *Farsighted: How we make the decisions that matter the most*. New York: Riverhead Books.

Johnson, S. (2018b, September 1). How to make a big decision. *The New York Times*. Accessed at www.nytimes.com/2018/09/01/opinion/sunday/how-make-big-decision .html on July 21, 2020.

Kahneman, D. (2011). *Thinking, fast and slow*. New York: Farrar, Straus and Giroux.

Kanter, R. M. (2012, September 25). Ten reasons people resist change. *Harvard Business Review*. Accessed at https://hbr.org/2012/09/ten-reasons-people-resist-chang on July 21, 2020.

Kaplan, R. S., & Norton, D. P. (2001). *The strategy-focused organization: How balanced scorecard companies thrive in the new business environment*. Boston: Harvard Business School Press.

Katzman, M. A. (2019). *Connect first: 52 simple ways to ignite success, meaning, and joy at work*. New York: McGraw-Hill.

Kegan, R., & Lahey, L. L. (2009). *Immunity to change: How to overcome it and unlock potential in yourself and your organization*. Boston: Harvard Business Review Press.

Keller, S., & Schaninger, B. (2019). *Beyond performance 2.0: A proven approach to leading large-scale change* (2nd ed.). Hoboken, NJ: Wiley.

Kelly, J. (2012, September–October). OctoPOTUS? *The University of Chicago Magazine*. Accessed at https://mag.uchicago.edu/law-policy-society/octopotus# on July 21, 2020.

Kethledge, R. M., & Erwin, M. S. (2017). *Lead yourself first: Inspiring leadership through solitude*. New York: Bloomsbury USA.

Kirby, J. (2010, January 1). The decade in management ideas. *Harvard Business Review*. Accessed at https://hbr.org/2010/01/the-decade-in-management-ideas on July 21, 2020.

Konnikova, M. (2020). *The biggest bluff: How I learned to pay attention, master the odds, and win*. New York: Penguin Press.

Kotter, J. P. (1995). Leading change: Why transformation efforts fail. *Harvard Business Review, 73*(2), 59–67.

Kotter, J. P. (2008). *A sense of urgency*. Boston: Harvard Business Press.

Kotter, J. P., & Cohen, D. S. (2012). *The heart of change: Real-life stories of how people change their organizations*. Boston: Harvard Business Review Press.

Kottler, J. A. (2014). *Change: What really leads to lasting personal transformation*. Oxford, England: Oxford University Press.

Kouzes, J. M., & Posner, B. Z. (2011). *Credibility: How leaders gain and lose it, why people demand it*. San Francisco: Jossey-Bass.

Kouzes, J. M., & Posner, B. Z. (2012). *The leadership challenge: How to make extraordinary things happen in organizations* (5th ed.). San Francisco: Jossey-Bass.

Lafley, A. G., Martin, R. L., Rivkin, J. W., & Siggelkow, N. (2012, September). Bringing science to the art of strategy. *Harvard Business Review*. Accessed at https://hbr.org/2012/09/bringing-science-to-the-art-of-strategy on July 21, 2020.

Lee, S. (2019, April 21). Why "find your passion" is such terrible advice. *The New York Times*. Accessed at www.nytimes.com/2019/04/21/smarter-living/why-find-your-passion-is-such-terrible-advice.html on July 21, 2020.

Livio, M. (2013). *Brilliant blunders: From Darwin to Einstein—Colossal mistakes by great scientists that changed our understanding of life and the universe*. New York: Simon & Schuster.

Lynch, M. (2016, September 18). *What you'd be surprised to learn about the 19th century's educational influence*. Accessed at www.theedadvocate.org/youd-surprised-learn-19th-centurys-educational-influence/ on October 18, 2020.

MacKay, J. (2019, January 17). *The myth of multitasking: The ultimate guide to getting more done by doing less* [Blog post]. Accessed at https://blog.rescuetime.com/multitasking/ on April 24, 2020.

MacKie, D. (2016). *Strength-based leadership coaching in organizations: An evidence-based guide to positive leadership development*. London: Kogan Page.

Malnight, T. W., Buche, I., & Dhanaraj, C. (2019, September–October). Put purpose at the core of your strategy. *Harvard Business Review*. Accessed at https://hbr.org/2019/09/put-purpose-at-the-core-of-your-strategy on July 21, 2020.

Mankins, M., & Garton, E. (2017). *Time, talent, energy: Overcome organizational drag and unleash your team's productive power*. Boston: Harvard Business Review Press.

Marcus, L. J., McNulty, E. J., Henderson, J. M., & Dorn, B. C. (2019). *You're it: Crisis, change, and how to lead when it matters most*. New York: PublicAffairs.

Marturano, J. (2014). *Finding the space to lead: A practical guide to mindful leadership*. New York: Bloomsbury Press.

McKeown, G. (2014). *Essentialism: The disciplined pursuit of less*. New York: Crown Business.

Miglani, B. (2013). *Embrace the chaos: How India taught me to stop overthinking and start living*. San Francisco: Berrett-Kohler.

Mlinarić, A., Horvat, M., & Smolčić, V. S. (2017). Dealing with positive publication bias: Why you should really publish your negative results. *Biochemia Medica, 27*(3), 447–452.

Mlodinow, L. (2018). *Elastic: Unlocking your brain's ability to embrace change*. New York: Vintage.

Modern living: Ozmosis in Central Park. (1976, October 4). *Time*. Accessed at http://content.time.com/time/magazine/article/0,9171,918412,00.html on November 3, 2020.

National Archives. (n.d.). *Vietnam War U.S. military fatal casualty statistics: Electronic records reference report*. Accessed at www.archives.gov/research/military/vietnam-war/casualty-statistics on July 22, 2020.

National Commission on Excellence in Education. (1983, April). *A nation at risk: The imperative for educational reform*. Washington, DC: U.S. Department of Education.

National Writing Project. (2009). *Steve Graham on the importance of learning to write well* [Video file]. Accessed at https://archive.nwp.org/cs/public/print/resource/2901 on July 21, 2020.

Nemeth, C. (2018). *In defense of troublemakers: The power of dissent in life and business*. New York: Basic Books.

Newport, C. (2012). *So good they can't ignore you: Why skills trump passion in the quest for work you love*. New York: Business Plus.

Newport, C. (2016a, February 18). A modest proposal: Eliminate email. *Harvard Business Review*. Accessed at https://hbr.org/2016/02/a-modest-proposal-eliminate-email on July 21, 2020.

Newport, C. (2016b). *Deep work: Rules for focused success in a distracted world*. New York: Grand Central.

Newport, C. (2019). *Digital minimalism: Choosing a focused life in a noisy world*. New York: Portfolio/Pengiun.

No Child Left Behind (NCLB) Act of 2001, Pub. L. No. 107-110, § 115, Stat. 1425 (2002).

O'Brien, S. (2019). *Why "follow your passion" is bad career advice*. Accessed at www.forbes.com/sites/susanobrien/2019/01/31/why-follow-your-passion-is-bad-career-advice/#5c13c2e442bd on July 22, 2020.

O'Donnell, R. (2018). *Preparing for change? Time to train your leaders*. Accessed at www.hrdive.com/news/preparing-for-change-time-to-train-your-leaders/539705/ on July 22, 2020.

Oettingen, G. (2014). *Rethinking positive thinking: Inside the new science of motivation*. New York: Current.

Onderick-Harvey, E. (2019, April 3). 5 ways to help your team be open to change. *Harvard Business Review*. Accessed at https://hbr.org/2019/04/5-ways-to-help-your-team-be-open-to-change on July 22, 2020.

Osborn, A. F. (1953). *Applied imagination: Principles and procedures of creative thinking*. New York: Scribner.

Oshin, M. (2018). *The Wilt Chamberlain effect: Why we make bad decisions, even when we know better*. Accessed at www.theladders.com/career-advice/the-wilt-chamberlain-effect-why-we-make-bad-decisions-even-when-we-know-better on July 22, 2020.

Peirce, E. (2017, July 6). *Why interviews are unreliable* [Blog post]. Accessed at https://blog.criteriacorp.com/why-interviews-are-unreliable/ on July 22, 2020.

Pentland, A. (2014). *Social physics: How good ideas spread—The lessons from a new science*. New York: Penguin Press.

Perkins, D. (1995). *Outsmarting IQ: The emerging science of learnable intelligence*. New York: Free Press.

Perry, A. M. (2019, May 17). *Students need more than an SAT adversity score, they need a boost in wealth* [Blog post]. Accessed at www.brookings.edu/blog/the-avenue/2019/05/17/students-need-more-than-an-sat-adversity-score-they-need-a-boost-in-wealth/ on July 22, 2020.

Peters, T. (2018). *The excellence dividend: Meeting the tech tide with work that wows and jobs that last*. New York: Vintage.

Peters, T., & Waterman, R. H., Jr. (1997). *In search of excellence: Lessons from America's best-run companies*. Thorndike, ME: G. K. Hall.

Pfeffer, J. (2015). *Leadership BS: Fixing workplaces and careers one truth at a time*. New York: Harper Business.

Pink, D. H. (2018). *When: The scientific secrets of perfect timing*. New York: Riverhead Books.

Pisano, G. P. (2019, January–February). The hard truth about innovative cultures. *Harvard Business Review*. Accessed at https://hbr.org/2019/01/the-hard-truth-about-innovative-cultures on July 22, 2020.

Pittampalli, A. (2016). *Persuadable: How great leaders change their minds to change the world*. New York: Harper Business.

Plummer, M., & Wilson, J. (2018, June 5). Become a more productive learner. *Harvard Business Review*. Accessed at https://hbr.org/2018/06/become-a-more-productive-learner on July 22, 2020.

Pondiscio, R. (2019). *How the other half learns: Equality, excellence, and the battle over school choice*. New York: Avery.

Porter, J. (2019, January 29). To improve your team, first work on yourself. *Harvard Business Review*. Accessed at https://hbr.org/2019/01/to-improve-your-team-first-work-on-yourself on July 22, 2020.

Presland, C. (2018, May 4). *"If you believe it, you can achieve it" is the worst possible success advice. Here's a better plan . . .* Accessed at https://medium.com/management-matters/why-if-you-believe-it-you-can-achieve-it-is-the-worst-possible-success-advice-and-whats-a-way-a5c78e735777 on November 11, 2020.

Quinn, R. E. (1996). *Deep change: Discovering the leader within.* San Francisco: Jossey-Bass.

Quote Investigator. (2014). *I would spend 55 minutes defining the problem and then five minutes solving it.* Accessed at https://quoteinvestigator.com/2014/05/22/solve/ on July 22, 2020.

Rath, T. (2007). *Strengths finder 2.0.* New York: Gallup Press.

Reeves, D. (2002). *The daily disciplines of leadership: How to improve student achievement, staff motivation, and personal organization.* San Francisco: Jossey-Bass.

Reeves, D. (2009). *Leading change in your school: How to conquer myths, build commitment, and get results.* Alexandria, VA: Association for Supervision and Curriculum Development.

Reeves, D. (2010, January 7). *The myth of buy-in* [Blog post]. Accessed at www.creativeleadership.net/resources-content/the-myth-of-buy-in on November 22, 2020.

Reeves, D. (2011). *Finding your leadership focus: What matters most for student results.* New York: Teachers College Press.

Reeves, D. (2016). *From leading to succeeding: The seven elements of effective leadership in education.* Bloomington, IN: Solution Tree Press.

Reeves, D. (2019, March 9). *Cheating our daughters: Four toxic messages behind the "good girl effect"* [Blog post]. Accessed at www.creativeleadership.net/blog/cheating-our-daughters on July 22, 2020.

Reeves, D. (2020a). *Achieving equity and excellence: Immediate results from the lessons of high-poverty, high-success schools.* Bloomington, IN: Solution Tree Press.

Reeves, D. (2020b, October 18). *How to stop the coming dropout time bomb* [Blog post]. Accessed at www.creativeleadership.net/blog/how-to-stop-the-coming-dropout-time-bomb on November 22, 2020.

Reeves, D. (2020c). *The learning leader: How to focus school improvement for better results* (2nd ed.). Alexandria, VA: Association for Supervision and Curriculum Development.

Reeves, D., & Allison, E. (2009). *Renewal coaching: Sustainable change for individuals and organizations.* San Francisco: Jossey-Bass.

Reeves, D., & Eaker, R. (2019). *100-day leaders: Turning short-term wins into long-term success in schools.* Bloomington, IN: Solution Tree Press.

Reeves, D., & Reeves, B. (2017). *The myth of the muse: Supporting virtues that inspire creativity*. Bloomington, IN: Solution Tree Press.

Reynolds, M. (2011, January 1). *Want to change? Get angry!* [Blog post]. Accessed at www.psychologytoday.com/us/blog/wander-woman/201101/want-change-get-angry on July 22, 2020.

Richmond, E. (2019, December 3). *No easy answers on PISA: U.S. scores flat in reading, math and science*. Accessed at www.ewa.org/blog-educated-reporter/no-easy-answers-pisa-us-flat-reading-math-and-science on October 18, 2020.

Richo, D. (2014). *The power of grace: Recognizing unexpected gifts on our path*. Boston: Shambhala.

Ries, E. (2019). *The leader's guide* [Audiobook]. Newark, NJ: Audible Studios.

Riggenbach, A., Goubert, L., Van Petegem, S., & Amouroux, R. (2019). Topical review: Basic psychological needs in adolescents with chronic pain—a self-determination perspective. *Pain Research and Management*. Accessed at https://doi.org/10.1155/2019/8629581 on November 17, 2020.

Rogelberg, S. G. (2019). *The surprising science of meetings: How you can lead your team to peak performance*. New York: Oxford University Press.

Rosling, H. (2018). *Factfulness: Ten reasons we're wrong about the world—And why things are better than you think*. New York: Flatiron Books.

Sanchez, P. (2018, December 20). The secret to leading organizational change is empathy. *Harvard Business Review*. Accessed at https://hbr.org/2018/12/the-secret-to-leading-organizational-change-is-empathy on July 22, 2020.

Satell, G. (2019, August 27). 4 tips for managing organizational change. *Harvard Business Review*. Accessed at https://hbr.org/2019/08/4-tips-for-managing-organizational-change?autocomplete=true on July 22, 2020.

Saunders, E. G. (2018, December 19). The 4 "attachment styles," and how they sabotage your work-life balance. *The New York Times*. Accessed at www.nytimes.com/2018/12/19/smarter-living/attachment-styles-work-life-balance.html on July 22, 2020.

Schneider, J. (2018, July 5). The problem with generalizing about "America's schools." *The Atlantic*. Accessed at www.theatlantic.com/education/archive/2018/07/americas-schools/564413/ on October 18, 2020.

Schoen, M. (2013). *Your survival instinct is killing you: Retrain your brain to conquer fear, make better decisions, and thrive in the 21st century*. New York: Hudson Street Press.

Schroeder, B. (2017). *Simply brilliant: Powerful techniques to unlock your creativity and spark new ideas*. New York: AMACOM.

Schulz, K. (2010). *Being wrong: Adventures in the margin of error*. New York: Ecco.

Schwartz, B. (2016). *The paradox of choice: Why more is less*. New York: Ecco.

Schwartz, T. (2012, July 11). Emotional contagion can take down your whole team. *Harvard Business Review*. Accessed at https://hbr.org/2012/07/emotional-contagion-can-ta on July 22, 2020.

Schwartz, T., & Pines, E. (2020, March 23). Coping with fatigue, fear, and panic during a crisis. *Harvard Business Review*. Accessed at https://hbr.org/2020/03/coping-with-fatigue-fear-and-panic-during-a-crisis on November 22, 2020.

Schwarz, R. M. (2013). *Smart leaders, smarter teams: How you and your team get unstuck to get results*. San Francisco: Jossey-Bass.

Scott, K. (2019). *Radical candor: Be a kick-ass boss without losing your humanity* (Fully revised and updated ed.). New York: St. Martin's Press.

Seligman, M. E. P. (2018). *The hope circuit: A psychologist's journey from helplessness to optimism*. New York: PublicAffairs.

Shambaugh, R. (2019, January 31). How to unlock your team's creativity. *Harvard Business Review*. Accessed at https://hbr.org/2019/01/how-to-unlock-your-teams-creativity on July 22, 2020.

Sharma, M. (2017). *Radical transformational leadership: Strategic action for change agents*. Berkeley, CA: North Atlantic Books.

Sharot, T. (2017). *The influential mind: What the brain reveals about our power to change others*. New York: Holt.

Siegler, M. G. (2015). *The app cleanse*. Accessed at https://500ish.com/the-app-cleanse-2f8096cecbd on July 22, 2020.

Simans. (2019). *Three ways to provoke new thinking*. Accessed at https://simans.org/three-ways-to-provoke-new-thinking/ on July 21, 2020.

Slavin, R. (2019, November 21). *On replicability: Why we don't celebrate Viking day* [Blog post]. Accessed at https://robertslavinsblog.wordpress.com/2019/11/21/on-replicability-why-we-dont-celebrate-viking-day/ on July 22, 2020.

Sloman, S., & Fernbach, P. (2017). *The knowledge illusion: Why we never think alone*. New York: Riverhead Books.

Snow, S. (2019, January 17). How to debate ideas productively at work. *Harvard Business Review*. Accessed at https://hbr.org/2019/01/how-to-debate-ideas-productively-at-work on July 22, 2020.

Spark. (n.d.). *Strategic growth plan: Spark's 10-year vision*. Accessed at https://sparkprogram.org/learn/our-organization/strategic-growth-plan/ on July 22, 2020.

Spitzer, D. R. (2019). *When measurement goes bad*. Accessed at www.amanet.org/articles/when-measurement-goes-bad/ on July 22, 2020.

Staats, B. R. (2018). *Never stop learning: Stay relevant, reinvent yourself, and thrive*. Boston: Harvard Business Review Press.

Step Change. (2019, February 1). *Why strategic plans fail: 5 things most leaders are missing* [Blog post]. Accessed at https://blog.hellostepchange.com/blog/why-strategic-plans-fail on July 22, 2020.

Stone, D., & Heen, S. (2014). *Thanks for the feedback: The science and art of receiving feedback well (even when it is off base, unfair, poorly delivered, and frankly, you're not in the mood).* New York: Viking.

Strategy. (n.d.). In *Merriam-Webster's online dictionary*. Accessed at www.merriam-webster.com/dictionary/strategy on July 21, 2020.

Strauss, V. (2012, December 23). The fundamental flaws of "value added" teacher evaluation. *The Washington Post*. Accessed at www.washingtonpost.com/news/answer-sheet/wp/2012/12/23/the-fundamental-flaws-of-value-added-teacher-evaluation/ on July 22, 2020.

Strauss, V. (2019, December 3). Expert: How PISA created an illusion of education quality and marketed it to the world. *The Washington Post*. Accessed at www.washingtonpost.com/education/2019/12/03/expert-how-pisa-created-an-illusion-education-quality-marketed-it-world/ on November 17, 2020.

Swaim, B. (2016, March 11). "Trust, but verify": An untrustworthy political phrase. *Washington Post*. Accessed at www.washingtonpost.com/opinions/trust-but-verify-an-untrustworthy-political-phrase/2016/03/11/da32fb08-db3b-11e5-891a-4ed04f4213e8_story.html on October 28, 2020.

Tasler, N. (2017, July 19). Stop using the excuse "Organizational change is hard." *Harvard Business Review*. Accessed at https://hbr.org/2017/07/stop-using-the-excuse-organizational-change-is-hard on July 22, 2020.

Taylor, B. (n.d.). *The 4 leadership styles, and how to identify yours*. Accessed at https://hbrascend.org/topics/4-leadership-styles-identify/ on July 22, 2020.

Taylor, W. C. (2016). *Simply brilliant: How great organizations do ordinary things in extraordinary ways*. New York: Portfolio/Penguin.

Temple, E. (2017, December 22). *The most-rejected books of all time*. Accessed at https://lithub.com/the-most-rejected-books-of-all-time/ on November 19, 2020.

Tierney, J., & Baumeister, R. F. (2019). *The power of bad: How the negativity effect rules us and how we can rule it*. New York: Penguin Press.

Turkle, S. (2015). *Reclaiming conversation: The power of talk in a digital age*. New York: Penguin Press.

Ulrich, D., Zenger, J., & Smallwood, N. (1999). *Results-based leadership*. Boston: Harvard Business School Press.

Venkataraman, B. (2019). *The optimist's telescope: Thinking ahead in a reckless age*. New York: Riverhead Books.

Vermeulen, F., & Sivanathan, N. (2017, November–December). Stop doubling down on your failing strategy. *Harvard Business Review*. Accessed at https://hbr.org/2017/11/stop-doubling-down-on-your-failing-strategy on July 22, 2020.

Wagner, R., & Harter, J. K. (2006). *12: The elements of great managing*. New York: Gallup Press.

Wald, M. L. (2000, July 7). Safety board blames pilot error in crash of Kennedy plane. *The New York Times*. Accessed at www.nytimes.com/2000/07/07/nyregion/safety-board-blames-pilot-error-in-crash-of-kennedy-plane.html on July 22, 2020.

Walker, M. (2020, September 22). Report cards: Reading continues to be a problem for Marion City Schools. *Marion Star*. Accessed at www.marionstar.com/story/news/2020/09/22/report-cards-reading-continues-problem-marion-schools/5807959002/ on November 17, 2020.

Weisinger, H., & Pawliw-Fry, J. P. (2015). *Performing under pressure: The science of doing your best when it matters most*. New York: Crown Business.

Welch, J. (2001). *Jack: Straight from the gut*. New York: Warner Books.

Wiens, K., & Rowell, D. (2018, December 31). How to embrace change using emotional intelligence. *Harvard Business Review*. Accessed at https://hbr.org/2018/12/how-to-embrace-change-using-emotional-intelligence on July 22, 2020.

Wiest, B. (2016). *101 essays that will change the way you think*. New York: Thought Catalog Books.

Wiseman, L. (2017). *Multipliers: How the best leaders make everyone smarter* (Revised and updated ed.). New York: HarperBusiness.

Wodtke, C. (2016). *Radical focus: Achieving your most important goals with objectives and key results*. Seattle, WA: Amazon.com Services.

Yaeger, D. (2016). *Great teams: 16 things high-performing organizations do differently*. Nashville, TN: W.

Young, S. (2017). *Stick with it: A scientifically proven process for changing your life—for good*. New York: HarperCollins.

Young, S. (2019). *Ultralearning: Timeless techniques for mastering hard skills*. New York: HarperBusiness.

Index

NUMBERS

A

B

C

D

I

J

K

L

M

N

O

U

100-Day Leaders
Douglas Reeves and Robert Eaker
Within 100 days, schools can dramatically increase student achievement, transform faculty morale, reduce discipline issues, and much more. Using *100-Day Leaders* as a guide, you will learn how to achieve a series of short-term wins that combine to form long-term success.
BKF919

From Leading to Succeeding
Douglas Reeves
Utilizing the crucial elements of effective leadership, education leaders can overcome the many challenges they face and learn the skills and characteristics they need to succeed. This book synthesizes research from 21st century sources and confronts prevalent leadership myths, while offering guidance on best leadership practices.
BKF649

Achieving Equity and Excellence
Douglas Reeves
Achieve high performance for all in your school. In *Achieving Equity and Excellence*, Douglas Reeves shares the mindset of high-poverty, high-success schools and outlines how to follow their example to make dramatic improvements to student learning, behavior, and attendance in a single semester.
BKF928

Time for Change
Anthony Muhammad and Luis F. Cruz
Exceptional leaders have four distinctive skills: strong communication, the ability to build trust, the ability to increase the skills of those they lead, and a results orientation. *Time for Change* offers powerful guidance for those seeking to develop and strengthen these skills.
BKF683